a passion for vegetables

a passion

PAUL GAYLER
for vegetables

Photography by Gus Filgate

The Lyons Press

To my family, friends and the many people in this exciting profession, who have inspired me over the years to truly enjoy the quality of good food.

First Lyons Press edition (c) 2000

ISBN 1-58574-536-7

The Lyons Press is an imprint of The Globe Pequot Press

Text © 1999 Paul Gayler
Photography © 1999 Gus Filgate
Designer: Paul Welti
Project editor: Kate Oldfield
Editor: Jane Middleton
Editorial assistant: Sheila Boniface
Home economists: Louise Pickford & Jane Stevenson
Stylist: Penny Markham

The Library of Congress Cataloging-in-Publication Data is available on file.

Printed and bound in Singapore by Tien Wah Press

contents

introduction

I have always believed that one of the hallmarks of a great restaurant is the care and attention it gives to its vegetables. The same could be said of the way we cook at home. All too often the cook's efforts are focused on producing meat or fish as the centerpiece of the meal and vegetables are not much more than an afterthought – boiled, then hastily tipped into a serving dish without much consideration for seasoning and presentation. Of course, it's hard to juggle the different elements of a meal and bring everything to the table at the same time in a state of perfection. Yet vegetables really do repay a little effort. Their natural flavors shine with just the minimum of encouragement – a sprinkling of chopped fresh mint on tender young peas or zucchini; a grating of nutmeg stirred into creamy mashed potatoes or lightly cooked spinach; a hint of oriental spicing with dark leafy greens such as curly kale or chard.

There's never been a more exciting time for vegetable cookery. Most supermarkets and vegetable stands stock an impressive range of vegetables throughout the year. Whether you want Chinese cabbage or Jerusalem artichokes, Spanish onions or Swiss chard, the chances are you'll be able to find them. But this very abundance can be confusing. Familiar varieties such as carrots and cabbage are often overlooked, while new imports can be mystifying for the uninitiated. In this book I have tried to come up with new ideas for vegetables that we take for granted – roasting cauliflower, for instance, in Cauliflower Aigredoux (see page 136) for a wonderfully nutty flavor; using beets in wickedly rich chocolate brownies (see page 162); stir-frying cucumber to make a spicy salad (page 27); or chargrilling green beans for a delectably smoky effect (see page 96). I have also applied traditional cooking techniques to less familiar vegetables to show how easy it is to incorporate them into everyday cooking: Japanese Artichoke and Arugula Soup (page 14), for example, or Butternut Squash and Orange Sorbet (page 164).

I grew up at a time when the rules of vegetable cookery were simple: you boiled them to death, then served them up in a soggy heap. My late mother was a good cook but, in common with most of her generation, she always boiled vegetables to a mush. I used to tease her: 'You eat the vegetables, Mum, I'll have the cooking liquid.' By the time I went to catering college, though, attitudes were changing – *nouvelle cuisine* chefs pioneered the *al dente* vegetable; the vegetarian movement was flourishing, inspiring much more creative vegetable dishes; and the first wave of exotic new imports began – eggplants, peppers, avocados, fennel, sweet potatoes, and others. My first job was at the Palace Hotel in Torquay, where I spent a year working on the vegetable section. I used to have to peel button onions by the bagful, and I lost count of the number of French beans I trimmed and peas I removed from their pods. I made silky-smooth vegetable purées of all colors – purple beets, glowing-orange carrot, pale, creamy celeriac – and painstakingly 'turned' vegetables (trimmed them into barrel shapes) to serve as garnishes. Despite the hard labor, this was where my love of vegetable cookery began, and when I moved to the Royal Garden Hotel in

London I was quite happy to be given the vegetable section again, catering for up to 700 covers daily and adding all manner of vegetable dishes to my repertoire.

Later, as chef director of Inigo Jones restaurant in Covent Garden, I offered a seven-course vegetarian menu alongside the regular menu – no one else was doing this at the time – and since then I have always taken an interest in vegetarian cooking, leading to my first book, *Virtually Vegetarian* (HarperCollinsPublishers, 1995). *A Passion for Vegetables* is not a vegetarian cookbook, although many of the recipes are suitable for vegetarians, or can easily be adapted. It is a celebration of all aspects of vegetable cookery. Originally I intended it to be a book of recipes for accompaniments, since this is where the potential of vegetables is most neglected nowadays, but it was impossible to resist the wider culinary role that vegetables can play – from soups and salads to main courses and even desserts.

Over the years I have travelled widely, discovering what the world's garden has to offer – both on holiday and working as a guest chef in Europe, the Far East, Mexico and the USA. So this book includes tastes and influences from around the world. Like many chefs cooking today, I have been seduced by the flavors of two very different regions, the Mediterranean and the Far East. Mediterranean food is so much a part of the British cookery scene now that everyone is familar with ingredients such as olives, garlic, arugula, basil and anchovies. But I like to look a little further afield for my Mediterranean fix: to the eastern side, where spices such as cinnamon, cumin, cardamom and saffron are more prevalent, and coriander leaves take over from basil or parsley as the herb of choice. One of the attractions of Mediterranean cookery for the vegetable enthusiast is the abundance of colorful, sun-ripened vegetables, which demand to be served up as dishes in their own right rather than as an accompaniment to meat or fish.

In Asian cooking, too, vegetables frequently take center stage: exotic leafy greens, including beautiful flowering cabbages; strange squashes and gourds; and the fabulous yard-long beans and yellow wax beans. I love to combine them with the punchy flavorings of this region – hot chiles, tamarind, *nam pla*, sesame oil, spices such as fenugreek, turmeric and star anise, and lots of fresh ginger, lemongrass and garlic.

Despite my passion for the foods I have come across abroad, it's good to return to the earthy, comforting flavors of home. There are some classic British vegetable dishes that I never tire of – light summery ones such as Simple Minted Summer Peas (see page 116), hearty root vegetable combinations like Scottish Rumbledethumps (see page 109), and My Mother''s Five-minute Onion Pudding (see page 108), a Sunday-lunch mainstay when I was a child.

Choosing Vegetables

You could say it's never been easier to choose vegetables. There they sit under the bright supermarket lights, their skins shiny, taut and blemish-free, and no matter what the time of year we can always find what the recipe demands. But although supermarkets have done an excellent job in making sure that fresh produce is always available to us, my instinct is still to go for vegetables grown in season, preferably locally, and picked as recently as possible. There are several advantages to shopping this way: first of all, seasonal vegetables taste much better: tomatoes, for example, that have been left to ripen on the vine, under the hot summer sun, are bursting with flavour – unlike insipid, hydroponically grown winter tomatoes that look good but taste of nothing. Secondly, if you buy in season the price is lower because there is an abundance of produce. Thirdly, seasonal vegetables produced locally rather than on the other side of the world haven't been sitting on ships or planes for days or even weeks, so they are fresher and their nutritional content should be higher.

Don't entirely discount frozen vegetables, however. Some of them, such as peas and fava beans, are frozen within minutes of picking and so in a sense are fresher than ones that have spent time in transit before being displayed in the shops for several days. Frozen vegetables can be a useful standby and are not to be despised.

For the cheapest and freshest vegetables, try pick-your-own farms for a pleasant day out and the chance to discover the difference in flavor between a shopbought vegetable and one that you've picked yourself that same day. Another good source is local markets, particularly the farmers' markets that are being set up all over the country (there are even plans to open one in north London shortly) and sell only goods that have been grown or produced locally. Some vegetables, of course, are unlikely to have been grown in the UK, and most large supermarkets now have reliable supplies of things such as chayote, chard and squashes that only a few years ago were unobtainable. But it's worth looking for these in ethnic shops such as Greek, Indian, Chinese or Caribbean grocers, too, where prices are often lower.

At the time of writing there has been a surge of interest in organic produce, due to concern about the effect of pesticides and other chemicals used in industrial farming on our health and the environment, and also because of the debate over genetically modified organisms (GMOs). If you wish to know more about the difference between organic and industrially produced food there are several good books available on the subject. Without getting involved in the pros and cons, I can say that as a chef my primary concern is that food should taste good, and organic vegetables, which have been grown slowly at their natural pace without any chemical imput, frequently have a better flavor. (This isn't always the case with imported out-of-season organic produce, however.) The best and often cheapest way to buy organic is to find a local source or to join one of the many box schemes (where a box of vegetables and/or fruit from a local supplier is delivered to your door). Remember that organic vegetables may not have the perfectly uniform appearance of non-organic produce, and why should they? Far better to buy for flavor than for looks – think of those wonderful Mediterranean markets with heaps of irregularly shaped fruit and vegetables that would probably never make the grade in your local supermarket but are ripe and fresh and bursting with flavor and vitality. Having said this, any vegetables, organic or otherwise, that are limp, withered or bruised – or, in the case of onions, garlic and potatoes, have begun to sprout – are past their best and should be avoided, if they're in the shops, or thrown out, if they're sitting in your larder.

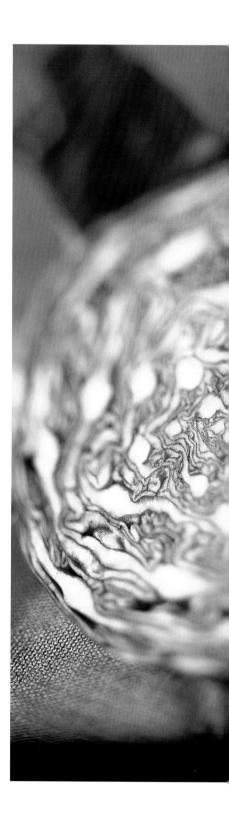

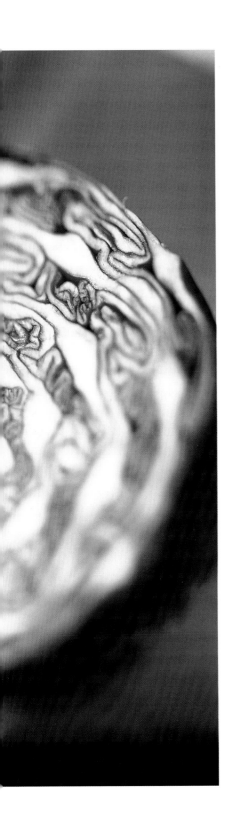

Wherever you buy your vegetables, it's important to store them properly once you get them home. In an ideal world, of course, they would all be eaten as fresh as possible but, failing that, most do very well in a cool (not too cold), dark, dry place such as the bottom of the fridge or a larder for a few days. A rough rule of thumb is that the harder the vegetable, the longer it will keep – so winter squashes, onions and most root vegetables should keep for several weeks; zucchini, eggplant and peppers for three or four days; and fragile salad leaves for only a day or two. Leafy vegetables should be kept in bags so they don't dry out and become limp. Don't wash vegetables until you are ready to use them, otherwise they may rot. Turn to the Glossary on page 170 for tips on storing and preparing more unusual vegetables.

Top Tips For Successful Vegetable Cookery

● **Remember, good cooking starts with good shopping. Always buy the best and freshest vegetables available and never compromise on quality.**

● **Prepare vegetables carefully and use good sharp knives to cut them so that they do not get bruised.**

● **Never leave prepared vegetables soaking in water before cooking. The vitamins will leach out and some vegetables become waterlogged.**

● **Season the cooking water well with salt. But don't use bicarbonate of soda as it increases vitamin C loss.**

● **Don't overcook vegetables when boiling them; the longer they are cooked, the more goodness is lost to the cooking water.**

● **Many cooks are afraid of high heat. A high heat achieves the best results for techniques such as roasting, chargrilling and stir-frying, sealing in flavor and nourishment.**

● **Give vegetable accompaniments the same attention and respect as you would the main course.**

● **When combining foods, do so in such a way that they bring out the best in each other, with contrasting but complementary tastes and textures.**

● **Don't be afraid to rely on a vegetable's natural flavors. A simple head of broccoli, for example, cooked to perfection, needs no embellishment.**

● **Be prepared to experiment. Trust your own instincts when it comes to taste.**

● **Remember, good presentation is also a vital ingredient.**

● **Be patient, organised and, most importantly, cook with love.**

Note: All recipes serve 4 unless otherwise stated.

roots & tubers

Root vegetables have sustained people through the long, hard winter months for centuries, providing valuable vitamins at a time when little other fresh food was available. Now that seasonal food scarcely exists any more, they no longer play such a vital role in our diet but they still make soothing, sustaining fuel when the nights turn dark and chilly. Whether transformed into hearty soups or slow-cooked casseroles, roasted to bring out their sweetness or turned into glorious mash, root vegetables are perfect comfort food – one of the pleasures of winter.

In spring and early summer we can enjoy tender new-season roots – tiny carrots, no more than a finger's

Jerusalem artichokes (left)

length; sweet, golfball-sized turnips and beets with their long, green leaves; and, best of all, new potatoes, of which Jersey Royals are the undisputed champions, best steamed or boiled with a sprig of mint and served simply with butter and sea salt.

Roots and tubers are amongst the most versatile of vegetables – carrots, sweet potatoes, even parsnips and beets, are equally at home in a cake or pudding as in a spicy stew. In fact in medieval times, when sugar was scarce, root vegetables were a welcome source of sweetness and were often made into dainty tarts and other sweet treats.

This homey-sounding group includes a few exotics. Jerusalem artichokes have become familiar over the last few years but Japanese artichokes (or crosnes), with their strange, spiral, seashell shape, are still a rarity, despite their exquisite flavor. Salsify and scorzonera, too, are little known in the UK, although in the rest of Europe these long, skinny brown roots are considered quite a delicacy from autumn to late spring.

Beets

Carrots

Celeriac

Japanese artichoke

Jerusalem artichoke

Parsnips

Potatoes

Radish (Mouli)

Rutabaga

Salsify

Sweet poatoes

Tard

Turnips

Yams

chapter **one**

Tastebuds are at their sharpest at the beginning of a meal so it's a good idea to serve up an appetizer with real impact. This doesn't have to be anything complicated - a simple assembly of ingredients with clear, well-defined flavors can be just as satisfying as more complex dishes. Vegetables really come into their own as appetizers, offering a variety of tastes and textures that are intriguing in their own right; they also make a perfect background for herbs, spices and other flavorings.

To make life easier for the cook, there are plenty of appetizers in this chapter that can be prepared in advance. Sometimes, though, it's fun to go for something really sensational, such as the Jerusalem Artichoke Soufflé on page 37 or the Cardoon Fritters with Parmesan Caper Aïoli on page 53.

Japanese Artichoke and Arugula Soup

1¹/₂ lbs. Japanese artichokes,
  trimmed
2 tablespoons unsalted butter
1 onion, finely chopped
3 cups vegetable stock
²/₃ cup milk
A good handful of arugula leaves,
  shredded
Freshly grated nutmeg
Salt and freshly ground black pepper

Japanese artichokes, or crosnes, are hard to find except from specialist vegetable markets. If you cannot obtain them, simply replace with Jerusalem artichokes.

Unless the Japanese artichokes are very young, blanch them in a large pot of boiling water for 10–15 seconds, drain well, then put them in a towel with a little coarse salt and rub gently to remove the skins.
  Heat the butter in a large saucepan, add the onion, then cover and sweat for 10 minutes, until soft. Add the artichokes and sweat for 5 minutes. Remove a cupful of the artichokes, cut any large ones in half and set aside.
  Add the stock and milk to the artichokes in the pan and bring to a boil. Reduce the heat and simmer for 20 minutes or until the artichokes are tender. Add the shredded arugula leaves and season with salt, pepper and nutmeg. Transfer to a blender and blitz to a light purée. Reheat the soup and check the seasoning. Stir in the reserved artichokes and serve immediately.

Potato and Goat's Cheese Soup
with White Truffle Oil

¹/₂ stick (¹/₄ cup) unsalted butter
³/₄ cup chopped onions
2²/₃ cups sliced leeks
1¹/₂ cups sliced potatoes (preferably
  new potatoes)
1 quart chicken stock, boiling
¹/₂ cup heavy cream
2 oz. mature goat's cheese,
  pushed through a wire strainer (to
  yield around ¹/₂ cup)
1 tablespoon white truffle oil
1 tablespoon snipped fresh chives
Salt and freshly ground black pepper

One of the greatest pleasures of being a chef is creating a new recipe. This soup is one of my earliest creations and remains a favorite. Try it and you won't be disappointed. Serve with lots of crusty French bread.

Heat the butter in a large saucepan, add the onions and leeks, then cover and cook gently for 8–10 minutes without coloring. Add the potatoes and sweat for 5 minutes. Stir in the boiling stock, then reduce the heat and simmer for 10–15 minutes until the potatoes are tender. Add 3 tablespoons of the cream and cook for 5 minutes longer.
  Mix the remaining cream with the goat's cheese and truffle oil and stir into the soup. Season to taste, sprinkle on the chives and serve immediately.

PG TIPS Variations on this soup are endless, I have successfully made it with fennel, cauliflower and salsify instead of potato.

Morel, Garlic
and Roasted Onion Broth

3 onions
8 garlic cloves
3 tablespoons vegetable oil
¹/₂ stick (¹/₄ cup) unsalted butter
1 teaspoon sugar
1 quart beef stock
5 tablespoons Madeira
5 oz. fresh morel mushrooms,
  cleaned (see page 172), or
  1 oz. dried morels, soaked in hot
  water for 30 minutes, then drained
4 thin slices of French bread
1 tablespoon chopped fresh parsley
Salt and freshly ground black pepper

A play on the traditional French onion soup, with a hint of earthiness from the morel mushrooms. Roasting the onions accentuates their flavor.

Preheat the oven to 425°F. Place the unpeeled onions and garlic cloves in a baking dish, pour over 2 tablespoons of the oil and roast for 20–25 minutes, until the garlic is soft. Remove the garlic from the dish, then return the onions to the oven and roast for a further 20–25 minutes, until dark golden and soft. Leave the onions to cool, then peel, cut in half and slice thinly. Heat the remaining oil and the butter in a pan, add the onions and sugar and sauté until caramelized.

Remove the onions from the pan and drain them. Place in a clean pot with the stock, Madeira and morels and bring to a boil. Reduce the heat and simmer for 20 minutes. Meanwhile, squeeze the garlic out of its skin and mash coarsely. Toast the French bread and spread with the garlic. Keep warm.

Season the soup to taste and ladle into serving bowls. Top each portion with a garlic croûton and sprinkle over the chopped parsley.

PG TIPS If you cannot find morels, replace them with field mushrooms.

'puréed corn
marries well
with crumbly
smoked
bacon'

Corn Bisque with Cheese and Smoked Bacon

3 corn on the cob
1¼ cups whole milk
2 tablespoons unsalted butter
1 onion, chopped
1 celery stalk, chopped
¼ cup all purpose flour
1¼ cups chicken or vegetable stock
1¼ cups grated Cheddar cheese
4-5 strips of smoked bacon, thinly sliced
Salt and freshly ground black pepper

Make this soup when fresh corn is at the height of its season. The bacon is added at the last minute to retain its crispness, the cheese allowed to melt on top of the soup.

Remove the husks from the corn, then hold each cob upright on a work surface and cut off the kernels with a knife. Put the corn kernels in a pan with the milk and bring to a boil. Reduce the heat and simmer for 10–15 minutes, until tender. Drain the corn and reserve the milk.

Melt the butter in a saucepan and gently sauté the onion and celery in it until soft. Add the flour, cook for 2–3 minutes over a low heat and then gradually stir in the milk and stock. Slowly bring to a boil, stirring all the time, until thickened. Reduce the heat and simmer for 15–20 minutes. Add the corn and half the cheese and cook very gently for 5 minutes, then pour into a blender and blitz to a purée. Reheat and season to taste.

Grill the bacon slices until crisp, then crumble them. Sprinkle the bacon over the soup with the remaining cheese just before serving.

PG TIPS Leeks or spinach would make good alternatives to the corn.

Iced Cucumber and Almond Soup

4 slices white country-style bread, crusts removed
1 cup blanched almonds
2 garlic cloves, peeled
1 quart vegetable stock
½ cucumber, peeled, seeded and chopped
½ cup olive oil
1 tablespoon sherry vinegar
¾ cup muscat grapes, halved and seeded
Salt

A chilled soup from the Andalucian region of Spain. The authentic recipe contains water rather than vegetable stock but I think the stock gives it more body.

Soak the bread in a little water, then put it in a blender or food processor with the almonds, garlic and some salt. Add a little of the stock and blitz until the almonds are finely ground.

Add the cucumber and then, with the motor running, gradually drizzle in the oil to form a light paste. Add the vinegar and the rest of the stock and blitz for 30 seconds. Transfer to the refrigerator. Serve well chilled, garnished with the grapes.

PG TIPS It is important that this soup is served very chilled. A few ice cubes may be added just before serving, but in certain parts of Spain this practice is frowned upon.

Spinach, Coconut Milk and Tapioca Soup

1/2 stick (1/4 cup) unsalted butter
1 1/4 lbs. fresh spinach,
   thoroughly washed
1 onion, roughly chopped
2 celery stalks, chopped
1 lemongrass stalk, chopped
1 in. piece of fresh ginger,
   finely chopped
1 red chile, chopped
2 cups chicken stock
14 fl. oz. can of unsweetened
   coconut milk
2 tablespoons tapioca
Freshly grated nutmeg
Salt and freshly ground black pepper

To garnish:
Thinly shredded scallions
Finely diced chile

A fragrant, oriental-inspired soup that makes a great opener to an informal barbecue lunch when served chilled.

Heat half the butter in a pot, add the spinach and cook, turning frequently with a wooden spoon, for 3–4 minutes, until it has wilted; cooking it any longer will dull its color. Drain the spinach, reserving the liquid, and set aside to cool. Heat the remaining butter in the pot, add the onion, celery, lemongrass, ginger and chile and cook over a gentle heat until slightly softened.

Pour in the stock and coconut milk and bring to a boil. Reduce the heat and simmer for 30 minutes, until the vegetables are tender. Transfer to a blender, add the spinach and reserved cooking liquid and blitz to a smooth purée.

Return the soup to a pot and bring back to a boil. Sprinkle in the tapioca, stirring constantly as it has a tendency to coagulate when added to hot liquid. Simmer for 6–8 minutes, then season with salt, pepper and nutmeg.

Serve hot or chilled, garnished with scallions and chile.

Leek, Watercress and Blue Cheese Vichysoisse

1 onion, chopped
3 leeks, chopped
1/2 stick (1/4 cup) unsalted butter
1 3/4 cups chopped new potatoes
1 quart vegetable or chicken stock
4 oz. bunch of watercress
5 tablespoons light cream
1/3 cup milk
3/4 cup crumbled Roquefort cheese
Salt and freshly ground black pepper

This is one of my favorite chilled soups. The cheese adds a little tanginess which blends well with the leek and peppery watercress.

Sweat the onion and leeks in the butter for about 5 minutes, until beginning to wilt. Add the potatoes and cook for 5 minutes longer. Add the stock and bring to a boil, then reduce the heat to a simmer and cook for 25 minutes, until all the vegetables are soft. Remove from the heat. Add the leaves from the bunch of watercress and leave to infuse in the pan for 5 minutes, then blitz to a smooth purée in a blender.

Put the cream, milk and Roquefort in a small pan and heat gently, stirring until smooth. Add to the soup, stir well together and add seasoning. Strain through a fine strainer, then chill until ready to serve.

Asparagus Consommé with Lemongrass

14 oz. asparagus

2 tablespoons unsalted butter

1 small onion, thinly sliced

1 small leek, white part only, sliced

2 lemongrass stalks, roughly
chopped

1 quart well-flavored chicken stock

3 egg whites

Salt and freshly ground black pepper

A consommé of great distinction. The flavor of lemongrass comes through beautifully. It is a great way to use up asparagus trimmings so nothing is wasted.

Peel the asparagus (see page 170) and keep the peelings. Cut off about 2 inches of each asparagus tip and set aside. Roughly chop the stalks. Heat the butter in a pan, add the onion and leek and cook over a low heat for 5–8 minutes, until tender. Add the asparagus peelings and stalks and the lemongrass and sweat for 5 minutes. Pour in the stock, bring to a boil, then reduce the heat and simmer for about 30–40 minutes.

Cook the asparagus tips in a pot of boiling water for 5 minutes, then drain, refresh under cold water and drain again. Cut into thin slices on the diagonal and set aside.

Strain the stock through a fine strainer and leave to cool. Next, clarify it as follows: lightly beat the egg whites just to break them up and then mix them into the stock. Pour into a large pot, bring gently to a boil and watch until the stock begins to bubble through the egg white crust that forms. Reduce the heat and simmer for about 10 minutes, until the soup begins to clear.

Place a large strainer lined with cheesecloth or a thin tea towel over a large bowl. Make a hole in the egg white crust and ladle the clear consommé through the strainer. Reheat and season to taste. Garnish with the asparagus tips and serve immediately.

PG TIPS Lemongrass is indispensable to Southeast Asian cooking, adding a fragrant, citrussy note to a wide variety of dishes. To prepare it, remove the tough outer layer and the fibrous upper part, then squash with the flat of a knife blade and chop finely.

Moroccan Carrot Soup with Chermoula

2 tablespoons unsalted butter

1/2 in. piece of fresh ginger, very

   finely chopped

1/4 teaspoon ground turmeric

1/4 teaspoon ground cumin

1 onion, chopped

1 leek, white part only, chopped

1 lb. carrots, cut into small

   chunks

1/4 teaspoon paprika

1 quart vegetable stock

Salt and freshly ground black pepper

For the chermoula:

4 1/2 oz. fresh coriander leaves (a

   good half-bunch)

1 garlic clove, crushed

1/4 teaspoon ground coriander

1/4 teaspoon ground cumin

1/2 cup olive oil

Juice of 1/4 lemon

Chermoula is the name given to a blend of herbs, spices, oil and lemon juice normally used as a marinade for fish or meat. In my variation it is more of a sauce. It will make far more than you need but you can use it in all manner of ways – as a salad dressing, for pasta or as a vibrant, zesty side sauce. Chermoula will keep in the fridge for 3–4 days but will lose its bright color after 2 days.

Heat the butter in a large pot, add the ginger, turmeric and cumin and sweat for 1–2 minutes. Add the onion, leek and carrots and sweat for 5 minutes. Stir in the paprika and then pour in the vegetable stock. Bring to a boil, then reduce the heat and simmer until the vegetables are tender, about 30 minutes. Purée in a blender until smooth, then reheat and season to taste.

For the chermoula, put all the ingredients in a blender and blitz to a smooth paste. Serve the soup in individual bowls, spooning about a tablespoon of chermoula over each portion.

PG TIPS Chermoula is an excellent marinade for fish or chicken but I also love it blended into a well-flavored mayonnaise, then spread on thick slices of bread and used to make a chicken, shrimp or tuna sandwich – sheer heaven!

'the vivid green of chermoula offsets the deep orange tones of this Moroccan-inspired soup'

Poivrade Artichokes
in Barigoule Cardamom Broth

16 poivrade artichokes (globe
    artichokes picked early, when still
    quite small – around 1^1/$_2$ in.
    diameter)
^{1}/$_4$ cup olive oil
4 small carrots, thinly sliced
2 small bay leaves
1 sprig of fresh thyme
2 small garlic cloves, crushed
1^1/$_4$ cups dry white wine
1^1/$_4$ cups water
1 teaspoon cardamom pods,
    cracked, black seeds removed
Juice of 2 small lemons
1 teaspoon coarse salt

This simple and delicous way to enjoy young artichokes was created by my friend the well-known chef Roger Vergé, at his restaurant Le Moulin de Mougins in the South of France. I have cheekily adapted it with a little infusion of cardamom, one of my favorite spices, which creates a delicate, spicy broth. Fennel and cauliflower are also good prepared this way.

Preheat the oven to 300°F. Prepare the artichokes by removing the stalks and trimming ^{1}/$_2$ inch off the tops of the leaves. As they are very young and tender, no other preparation is required.

Heat the olive oil in a flameproof casserole dish, add the artichokes and sauté over a gentle heat for a few minutes without letting them brown. Add all the remaining ingredients and bring to a boil. Reduce the heat, cover with a tight-fitting lid or with foil and transfer to the oven. Braise for about 20–30 minutes or until the artichokes are tender.

Drain, reserving the cooking liquid. Boil the liquid until reduced by about a third, then return the artichokes to the liquid and leave to cool. Serve at room temperature.

Blackened Acorn Squash and Sorrel Soup

^{1}/$_2$ stick (^{1}/$_4$ cup) unsalted butter
1 onion, chopped
1 tablespoon Cajun spices
1 acorn squash, peeled, seeded
    and cut into small chunks
4-5 strips bacon, cut into
    small dice
3 cups chicken stock
^{2}/$_3$ cup heavy cream
1 large potato, cut into small chunks
2 garlic cloves, crushed
^{1}/$_2$ in. piece of fresh ginger,
    grated
A handful of sorrel leaves
Salt and freshly ground black pepper

An unusual soup, made with roasted squash and Cajun spices roasted together until blackened. Cajun spices are a commercial blend of dry spices usually consisting of paprika, coriander, garlic powder, chili and cumin.

Preheat the oven to its highest setting. Heat the butter in a shallow casserole dish, add the onion and Cajun spices and cook for 5 minutes. Add the acorn squash and toss to coat with the spices. Place in the hot oven for 10–12 minutes, then turn the pieces of squash. Add the bacon and cook for 10–15 minutes, until everything is evenly charred.

Transfer the mixture to a large pot, add the stock, cream, diced potato, garlic and ginger and bring to a boil. Reduce the heat and simmer for 30 minutes. Blitz in a blender until smooth, then return to the pot and reheat gently. Tear the sorrel leaves into the soup in smallish pieces and stir until wilted. Taste and adjust the seasoning, then serve.

Roasted Tomato and Pineapple Mint Sorbet

3 lb. ripe plum tomatoes
2¹/₄ cups confectioners sugar
¹/₂ cup water
1 tablespoon lemon juice
A dash of Tabasco
1 tablespoon chopped fresh
  pineapple mint, plus a few leaves
  to decorate

This full-flavored tomato sorbet makes an ideal appetizer on a hot summer's day. I like to serve it with fresh tuna carpaccio or shrimp in a spicy, cocktail-style sauce, or just on its own. Make sure the tomatoes you buy are perfectly ripe.

Preheat the oven to 400°F. Cut the tomatoes in half and remove the seeds. Place the tomatoes cut-side down on a baking sheet and roast for 10–15 minutes, then transfer to a wire rack and leave to cool. When cool, peel them carefully and remove the central cores.

Put the sugar and water in a pan, bring to a boil and boil for 1 minute. Place the tomatoes in a blender, pour on the sugar syrup, then add the lemon juice, Tabasco and pineapple mint, and blitz until smooth. Pour into a bowl and refrigerate until thoroughly chilled. Pour into a sorbetière and freeze until firm, following the manufacturer's instructions. If you don't have a sorbetière, pour the mixture into a bowl and place in the freezer. After 30 minutes, when the mixture is beginning to set, remove it from the freezer and beat well with an electric beater or hand blender to disperse any ice crystals, then return it to the freezer. Repeat this 2 or 3 times, then leave until the sorbet is set firm. Serve decorated with pineapple mint leaves.

PG TIPS If you cannot get pineapple mint, use ordinary mint.

shoots & thistles

This category includes two of the oddballs of the vegetable world: huge, silver-tinged, spiky cardoons and swollen globe artichokes in their impenetrable-looking suits of armour. Artichokes have long been considered a delicacy and the whole delicious ritual of eating them – pulling off the leaves one by one, dipping them into a light sauce, and finally devouring the tender, meaty heart – is a reminder that fast food is not the Holy Grail of eating after all; some tastes are worth savoring.

If artichokes are the star, cardoons are the poor relation (like artichokes, they are a kind of thistle, except it is the stalks that are eaten rather than the heads). They have

Baby Fennel (left)

never achieved the popularity of the artichoke and are only really valued in parts of the Mediterranean and Africa. Yet they are easy to cultivate and they have a delicious mild and subtle flavor.

Personally I believe the finest delicacies come from the vegetable world: globe artichokes, truffles, wild mushrooms, tiny new-season peas and, of course, the ultimate early-summer luxury – fresh asparagus. This elegant member of the lily family has been considered the king of vegetables since Roman times, although anyone who has eaten only the tasteless, tired-looking stems available out of season may wonder why. Fresh, juicy spears, eaten on the day they are picked, are an unrivalled treat. If you are ever lucky enough to find wild asparagus, its intense, slightly bitter flavor is wonderful with scrambled eggs.

Fennel and celery are two shoots that look as if they should be related but in fact have very little in common except their Italian background (cultivated celery was developed from the wild herb by the Italians in the sixteenth century). With its remarkable licorice flavor, fennel is one of the most distinctive of vegetables but it is never overpowering. Celery, on the other hand, lacks subtlety and should be used with some discretion – or munched raw in order to enjoy its juicy crunch.

Asparagus

Baby Fennel

Cardoons

Celery

Fennel

Globe artichokes

Poivrade artichokes

Palm hearts

Caramelized Young Garlic and Parsley Soup

2 tablespoons unsalted butter
20 new-season garlic cloves, peeled
2 tablespoons white wine vinegar
2/3 cup milk
2 1/2 cups well-flavored chicken
   stock
3 slices of white bread
5 tablespoons light cream
1 tablespoon coarsely chopped fresh
   flat-leaf parsley
Salt and freshly ground black pepper

If you love garlic, as I do, here is a simple, strongly perfumed soup, packed with flavor. It is a variation on a recipe from a leading American chef, my friend Susan Spicer, of Bayona Restaurant in New Orleans. Serve with chunks of bread for dipping.

Heat the butter in a deep pot. When it begins to foam, add the garlic cloves and reduce the heat to low. Cook, turning occasionally, until the cloves are golden brown and caramelized, bringing out their natural sugars. This will take about 20 minutes and the cloves will be almost puréed by the end. Add the vinegar and boil until completely evaporated.

Pour in the milk and chicken stock, bring to a boil, then reduce the heat and simmer for 15 minutes. Roughly tear in the bread, and remove from the heat.

Blitz the soup in a blender until smooth, then strain through a fine strainer and return to the pot. Reheat, season to taste and stir in the cream and parsley.

PG TIPS You could vary this soup by adding some walnuts or cannellini beans with the milk and stock.

Cauliflower, Mussel and Anise Saffron Soup

2 1/4 lb. fresh mussels, scrubbed
   and debearded
1/2 cup dry white wine
1 1/4 cups water
2 tablespoons unsalted butter
1 onion, chopped
1 cauliflower, cut into flowerets
1/2 teaspoon mild curry powder
1/2 teaspoon saffron strands
2 1/2 cups light chicken stock
1/2 cup light cream
1/4 cup anise liquor, such as
   Pernod or Ricard
1 tablespoon chopped fresh dill

Put the mussels in a large pot with the white wine and water, place over a high heat and boil for 2–3 minutes, covered, until the shells just open, shaking the pot from time to time. Do not overcook or they will become rubbery. Leave to cool, then discard any mussels that have remained closed and shell the rest. Drain off the liquor through a fine strainer.

Heat the butter in a pot, add the onion, and sweat for 10–12 minutes. Add the cauliflower and curry powder and sweat for 5 minutes, then add the saffron. Pour in the stock and the cooking liquid from the mussels. Bring to a boil, then simmer for about 20 minutes or until the cauliflower is well cooked. Pour into a blender and blitz until smooth. Return to the pot and add the cream, anise, dill and shelled mussels. Heat gently but do not boil. Serve straight away.

PG TIPS When cleaning mussels, throw away any that are open as this usually means they are dead. However, tap an open one on a work surface or press it lightly; if it closes it is fine (it was just popping out for a look around!).

Spicy Cauliflower and Tomato Salad

1 large cauliflower, divided into flowerets
2 scallions, shredded
1 red onion, finely chopped
1 tablespoon snipped fresh chives

For the dressing:
1 red pepper
1 beefsteak tomato
2 red Serrano chiles
1/2 onion, peeled
3 tablespoons olive oil
Juice of 2 limes
1/2 cup orange juice
3 tablespoons tomato juice
Tabasco, to taste
1 tablespoon sugar

Other vegetables such as artichokes, asparagus and fennel can be used instead of the cauliflower. You can leave out the Tabasco sauce if you don't like your food too spicy.

For the dressing, brush the red pepper, tomato, chiles and onion with the oil and charbroil them for about 30 minutes, until well charred (alternatively, put them in a baking dish, pour over the oil and roast in a hot oven).

Cut the pepper and tomato in half and remove the seeds. Chop the chiles and the onion. Place in a blender with all the remaining dressing ingredients and purée until smooth. Pass through a coarse strainer into a bowl.

Cook the cauliflower flowerets in boiling salted water for 2 minutes, until just tender but still firm. Drain well and add to the dressing immediately. Leave to cool. Serve lightly chilled or at room temperature, sprinkled with the scallions, red onion and chives.

PG TIPS The secret of this recipe is to add the cauliflower to the marinade while it is hot, to allow the dressing to soak in and give maximum flavor.

Hot Chili Cucumber Salad

2 tablespoons vegetable or peanut oil
1 tablespoon sesame oil
1 garlic clove, crushed
1 in. piece of fresh ginger, very finely chopped
1 tablespoon Asian sweet chili sauce
1 large cucumber, peeled, halved lengthways, seeded and cut into slices 1/2 in. thick
1 tablespoon ketjap manis (Indonesian soy sauce)
1/2 teaspoon sugar
Salt

The thought of a hot cucumber salad may not be to everyone's liking but try it before you make a final judgement! Ketjap manis is a thick, licorice-flavored soy sauce made from molasses, spices, herbs and sugar. It gives a sweet flavor I just love.

Heat both oils in a wok, add the garlic and ginger and stir-fry for 30 seconds. Add the chili sauce and cucumber and cook for a further 2 minutes. Finally, add the ketjap manis and sugar and toss to glaze. Taste and add salt if necessary. Serve warm or at room temperature, but not cold.

'my version
of spinach
salad'

Spinach Salad with Crisp Prosciutto and Goat's Cheese Dressing

**8 thin slices of prosciutto, about
    4¹/₂ oz. in total**
³/₄ lb. young spinach leaves
**³/₄ cup thinly sliced button
    mushrooms**
**2 eggs, hardboiled and
    roughly chopped**

For the dressing:
3 oz. mild goat's cheese
1 tablespoon sherry vinegar
3 tablespoons light cream
¹/₂ cup olive oil
1 teaspoon Dijon mustard
1 teaspoon fresh thyme leaves
Salt and freshly ground black pepper

Since the early days of *nouvelle cuisine*, when the Troisgros brothers created the spinach salad, many chefs have come up with variations on the theme. Why should I be different? Here's mine! The spinach is tossed in a creamy goat's cheese dressing and topped with crisp prosciutto.

For the dressing, blitz together the goat's cheese, vinegar, cream, olive oil, mustard and thyme in a blender or food processor until light and creamy. Season to taste with salt and plenty of black pepper.

Place the prosciutto slices under a hot broiler until crisp on one side, then turn them over and broil until crisp on the other side. Drain on paper towels.

Put the spinach, mushrooms and chopped hardboiled eggs in a bowl and gently toss with the dressing. Top with the broiled prosciutto.

Barbecued Patty Pan Salad

16 green patty pan squash
16 yellow patty pan squash
¹/₄ cup virgin olive oil
1 tablespoon balsamic vinegar
1 garlic clove, crushed
12 fresh mint leaves
12 fresh basil leaves
¹/₂ teaspoon Dijon mustard
2 tablespoons pine kernels, toasted
**1¹/₂ cups fresh Parmesan cheese,
    cut into shavings**
Salt and freshly ground black pepper

The ideal salad for a summer barbecue. The balsamic, herb and garlic dressing is perfect with the smoky squash.

Cut the patty pan squash in half vertically, brush them with half the oil and cook on a barbecue (or a ridged grill pan) until lightly charred and just tender.

In a large bowl, mix together the remaining oil, balsamic vinegar, garlic, herbs and mustard and season to taste. Add the grilled squash to the bowl and leave to marinate at room temperature for 2–3 hours, tossing occasionally.

Transfer to a serving dish, scatter over the pine kernels and Parmesan and serve.

PG TIPS You could replace the Parmesan with chunks of salty Greek feta.

Snow peas and Artichoke Salad
with Orange and Mustard Dressing

1/2 lb. poivrade artichokes (globe artichokes picked when still quite small – about 1 1/2 in. diameter)
1/4 lb. Jerusalem artichokes
1/2 lb. snow peas

For the dressing:
Zest of 1/2 orange, cut into long shreds
Juice of 1/2 orange
1 teaspoon wholegrain mustard
1 1/2 tablespoons champagne vinegar
2 1/2 tablespoons virgin olive oil
1/4 cup walnut oil
Salt and freshly ground black pepper

There is nothing to beat this crisp, fruity salad. Serve it as a dinner-party knockout or just a lazy weekend treat.

Prepare the poivrade artichokes by removing the stalks and trimming 1/2 in. off the tops of the leaves. As they are very young and tender, no other preparation is required.

Peel the Jerusalem artichokes. Cook the poivrade and Jerusalem artichokes in separate pots of boiling salted water for 8–10 minutes or until tender, then drain. Blanch the snow peas in boiling water for 2 minutes. Drain and refresh under cold water, then drain again.

For the dressing, blanch the orange zest in boiling water for 1 minute, then refresh under cold water and drain well. Whisk together all the dressing ingredients, adding seasoning to taste.

Place the artichokes in a bowl, pour over the dressing, then add the snow peas. Serve at room temperature.

PG TIPS Store oils in a cool, dark place, date them and use within three months of opening. I keep walnut and hazelnut oils, both highly perishable, in the fridge. I never refrigerate olive oil, however, as the cold destroys its delicate flavor.

Truffle Potato Salad
with Warm Pesto Dressing

1 lb. truffle potatoes
1/2 cup virgin olive oil
2 garlic cloves, peeled
2 tablespoons pine kernels
3 oz. fresh basil leaves
2 tablespoons freshly grated Parmesan cheese
A pinch of sugar
Salt and freshly ground black pepper

A sexy potato salad with colors to set the tastebuds dancing in anticipation. Purple truffle potatoes (sometimes sold as black potatoes) are becoming increasingly available now but any variety of firm, waxy potato could be used instead.

Steam or boil the potatoes in their skins until just tender, about 15–20 minutes. Drain well and leave until cool enough to handle. Meanwhile, warm the olive oil in a saucepan with the garlic for 2–3 minutes to infuse the oil, then add the pine kernels and basil and leave over a low heat for a further 2–3 minutes. Place in a blender and blitz until smooth. Mix in the Parmesan and season with the sugar, salt and ground black pepper.

Peel the potatoes and place in a warm salad bowl. Pour the warm pesto dressing over the potatoes and serve immediately.

'purple
potatoes
with
summer
basil - a
feast for
the eyes'

'the heady aniseed flavors of fennel meld superbly with garlic-infused olive oil'

Mediterranean-style Fennel

12-16 baby fennel bulbs (or 4
　ordinary fennel bulbs, cut into
　quarters)
1/4 cup olive oil
4 garlic cloves, peeled
1 bay leaf
1/2 cup dry white wine
1/2 cup water
8 large scallions, cut into 2 in.
　lengths
4 ripe but firm plum tomatoes,
　skinned, seeded and cut into
　quarters
1 tablespoon chopped fresh oregano
1/2 cup meat stock
12 fresh purple basil leaves
A little lemon juice
Salt and freshly ground black pepper

Fennel is a spectacular vegetable, with a distinguished appearance and a flavor to match. It is best appreciated in the Mediterranean, especially Italy, France and North Africa. Here is a delicate Mediterranean-style preparation, full of the region's sun-drenched flavors.

Remove the fronds from the fennel and trim the bulbs. Heat the olive oil in a shallow pan, add the fennel and whole garlic cloves and sauté for 5 minutes. Add the bay leaf, white wine and water and bring to a boil, then reduce the heat and simmer for 10 minutes. Add the scallions, cover the pan and cook for 15 minutes. Remove the lid, add the tomatoes, oregano and stock and cook over a gentle heat for 5 minutes. Finally stir in the purple basil, add a squeeze of lemon juice and season with salt and pepper. Serve immediately.

PG TIPS A little thinly sliced raw fennel adds a subtle flavor to many cold dishes, such as a simple mixed salad, and is also good served with salmon carpaccio, a particular favorite of mine.

Porcini Carpaccio with White Truffle Oil and Parmesan

1 lb. large, very fresh porcini
　mushrooms (see page 172)
3 tablespoons lemon juice
6 tablespoons virgin olive oil
1 teaspoon white truffle oil
1/2 garlic clove, sliced
1 teaspoon chopped fresh mint
3 oz. fresh Parmesan cheese,
　cut into shavings (around 1 1/2 cups)
Sea salt and freshly ground black
　pepper

A classical carpaccio, named after a famous Venetian renaissance painter, is made with very thinly sliced raw beef. Here I have used the term for thinly sliced vegetables (or salmon, see Tips above).

Using a mandoline or very sharp knife, thinly slice the cleaned porcini. Whisk together the lemon juice, both oils, garlic and mint and season to taste.

Drizzle a tablespoon of the dressing on each of 4 serving plates, then arrange the porcini slices on top, overlapping them attractively. Spoon over the remaining dressing, season with salt and pepper and finally scatter over the Parmesan shavings. Serve with crusty bread.

PG TIPS To make Parmesan shavings, I find it best to use a swivel-bladed potato peeler. The shavings should be prepared at the last moment for the best results.

Stuffed Zucchini with Goat's Cheese, Yellow Tomato Sauce Vierge

8 small to medium zucchini, about 1 in. thick

¼ cup olive oil

2 shallots, chopped

1 garlic clove, crushed

1 teaspoon chopped fresh oregano

1 teaspoon chopped fresh thyme

¼ lb. firm goat's cheese, crumbled (around 1 cup)

2 tablespoons fresh white bread-crumbs

Salt and freshly ground black pepper

For the sauce vierge:

⅔ cup olive oil

2 garlic cloves, crushed

¾ lb. yellow tomatoes, finely diced (around a generous cup)

5 tablespoons balsamic vinegar

6 fresh basil leaves

Colorful, light and delicate, this is a real summer treat. The stuffed zucchini can be prepared in advance and broiled when needed. They can also be baked in the oven if you prefer, although they will take a little longer to cook.

Slice the ends off the zucchini and, using an apple corer, carefully remove the center of each zucchini to leave a hollow tube. Chop the zucchini flesh into small dice.

Heat half the oil in a pan, add the shallots, garlic and diced zucchini, then cover and sweat for 5–8 minutes, until tender. Stir in the herbs and turn the mixture into a bowl. Add the goat's cheese, breadcrumbs and some seasoning and mix well to form a firm stuffing. Place the stuffing in a piping bag and carefully fill each zucchini. Brush them with the remaining oil and cook under a preheated broiler or on a ridged broiler pan for 12–15 minutes, turning regularly, until tender and lightly charbroiled.

Meanwhile, for the dressing, heat the oil over a low heat, add the garlic and cook gently until softened, about 5–8 minutes. Add the yellow tomatoes, vinegar and basil and leave over a low heat to infuse for 5 minutes. Season to taste.

Arrange the broiled zucchini in a serving dish, pour over the sauce and serve. They are equally delicious warm or cold.

PG TIPS The stuffing is very versatile and can be used for other vegetables, such as baked tomatoes and small egg-plants, or as a filling for ravioli and cannelloni.

'a contrasting
blend of
textures:
creamy
goat's cheese
with crisp zuc-
chini'

Young Leeks and Asparagus
with Truffle Gribiche

**1 lb. tender young leeks, cut
into 4 in. lengths**

**³/₄ lb. young asparagus,
trimmed (see page 170) and tied
together with string**

For the truffle gribiche:

3 tablespoons olive oil

**1 tablespoon champagne vinegar (or
tarragon vinegar)**

1 teaspoon Dijon mustard

**3 eggs, hardboiled and
chopped**

**1 teaspoon superfine capers, well
drained**

**¹/₂ teaspoon finely chopped fresh
truffle**

**2 teaspoons chopped mixed fresh
herbs, such as parsley, tarragon
and chervil**

A pinch of sugar

Salt and freshly ground black pepper

Bring 5 cups of water to the boil in a stainless steel pot, add the leeks and cook for 3 minutes over a gentle heat. Remove with a slotted spoon and leave to cool. Bring the water back to a boil, add the asparagus and cook for 3 minutes. Remove with a slotted spoon and drain well. When the leeks are cool enough to handle, squeeze them lightly to extract any remaining liquid. Place in a shallow dish with the asparagus.

For the gribiche, mix together the oil, vinegar and mustard. Add the eggs, capers, truffle and herbs and season with the sugar, salt and pepper. Spoon the gribiche over the leeks and asparagus and leave to cool to room temperature before serving.

PG TIPS For perfect hardboiled eggs, begin by piercing the raw eggs once at the rounded end (where there is an air space) with a pin. This will make it easier to shell them once they are cooked. Cook the eggs in water at a gentle boil for 8–10 minutes, then refresh with cold water until completely cool and shell them.

Escalivada (Toasted Catalan Vegetables)

4 eggplants
4 red peppers
1/2 cup virgin olive oil
1 tablespoon superfine capers, well
   drained
12 black olives
2 garlic cloves, thinly sliced
Salt

The word escalivada comes from the term 'to toast over a flame'. Sometimes onions and tomatoes are added and the vegetables baked for convenience. Either way, the smoky flavors of the dish pervade it.

Preheat a charcoal grill or ridged grill pan until hot. Brush the eggplants and peppers with a little of the oil and grill for 15–20 minutes, turning occasionally, until charred all over and tender. Place the peppers in a bowl, cover with plastic wrap and leave for 5 minutes; this makes them easier to peel. Peel the peppers and cut into strips 3/4 in. thick. Cut the eggplants into slices 1/2 in. thick.

Arrange the peppers and eggplants in a serving dish and season with salt. Sprinkle over the capers and olives, then the garlic. Drizzle over the remaining olive oil. Serve warm or at room temperature.

PG TIPS Add some goat's cheese or feta before serving for a salty flavor to contrast with the sweet pepper.

Jerusalem Artichoke Soufflés

1/2 stick (1/4 cup) unsalted butter
A little freshly grated Parmesan
   cheese
1 lb. Jerusalem artichokes,
   peeled and cut into small pieces
2/3 cup water
1/4 cup all purpose flour
2/3 cup milk
4 eggs, separated
Cayenne pepper
Salt and freshly ground black pepper

These are a wonderful appetizer for a special occasion. Jerusalem artichokes have an earthy, nutty flavor that makes a great soufflé.

Preheat the oven to 400°F and place a baking sheet in it. Use half the butter to grease four 1-cup soufflé dishes and then dust them with Parmesan.

Put the artichokes in a pan with the water, cover and bring to a boil. Simmer for 10–15 minutes, until tender. Drain, reserving the cooking water, and mash the artichokes to a purée. Place the purée in a clean pan and stir over a very low heat to dry it out.

Melt the remaining butter in a pan, stir in the flour and cook gently for a few minutes. Gradually stir in the milk and the reserved cooking liquid, then bring to a boil, stirring all the time, so the sauce thickens. Remove from the heat and add the artichoke purée, then the egg yolks. Season generously with salt, pepper and cayenne. Beat the egg whites until stiff. Beat one third of the whites into the purée mixture, then fold in the rest. Fill the soufflé dishes with the mixture, place on a baking sheet and bake for 20–25 minutes, until puffed and golden but still slightly creamy in the center. Serve immediately.

'when broken, the soft egg yolk suffuses the basil butter'

Baked Artichokes
with Coddled Eggs Niçoise

4 medium to large globe artichokes
2 tablespoons unsalted butter
1/2 cup dry white wine
2/3 cup water
4 large eggs
2/3 cup heavy cream
2 plum tomatoes, skinned, seeded
**   and cut into small dice**
8 fresh basil leaves, roughly chopped
Salt and freshly ground black pepper

Baking eggs inside vegetable shells is not a new idea but it does make for a rather dramatic presentation.

With a large, sharp knife, slice one third off the top of each artichoke. Pull off the outer leaves and discard them. Break the artichoke stems at the base, then trim about 1/4 in. from the base.

Use the butter to grease a flameproof casserole just large enough to hold the artichokes. Place the artichokes in it and pour over the wine and water. Bring to a boil, then reduce the heat, cover and cook gently for 15–20 minutes or until just tender; test the base of each artichoke with the point of a knife. Remove the artichokes from the flameproof casserole, reserving the cooking liquid, and leave them to cool, placed upside down to drain off any liquid.

Preheat the oven to 400°F. To create a central cavity in each artichoke, pull out the small inner leaves, then use a teaspoon to scrape out the fibrous choke. Place the artichokes in a baking dish and crack an egg into the center of each one. Season generously with salt and pepper and bake in the oven for 5 minutes or until the eggs are lightly set. Meanwhile, make the sauce: reheat the cooking liquid, then add the cream and boil for 5 minutes. Stir in the tomatoes and basil and season to taste.

Place each artichoke on a serving plate, coat lightly with the sauce and serve immediately.

Beet Tzatziki

1 cup Greek yoghurt (or thick whole
**   milk yoghurt)**
3 medium size cooked beets,
**   peeled and grated**
3 garlic cloves, crushed
2 tablespoons chopped fresh dill
2 tablespoons good-quality red wine
**   vinegar**
2 tablespoons light olive oil
Salt and freshly ground black pepper

Tzatziki is a Greek sauce made with yoghurt and cucumber. Here I use grated beets, which have a wonderful color and make a refreshing change – an idea I got from a recent visit to Crete. Serve as an accompaniment to deep-fried artichokes or asparagus. It also makes an interesting relish for smoked salmon or a simple dip for raw vegetables.

Place the yoghurt in a bowl, add the beets, garlic and dill and mix well. Stir in the vinegar and olive oil and season to taste. Refrigerate until ready to use.

Porcini 'Under Oil'

3/4 cup virgin olive oil

3/4 lb. fresh porcini
   mushrooms, wiped clean with a
   damp cloth and thickly sliced

2 shallots, thinly sliced into rings

2 garlic cloves, crushed

6 fresh sage leaves

4 plum tomatoes, skinned, seeded
   and cut into large pieces

12 black olives

1/2 cup dry white wine

Juice of 1 lemon

Salt and freshly ground black pepper

The Italians have been preserving vegetables in oil for centuries. Not only is it a good method of keeping them, it also enhances their flavors. Make this recipe when fresh porcini come into season so you can enjoy them throughout the year. Eggplants can be prepared the same way.

Heat 2 tablespoons of the olive oil in a large pot, add the porcini, shallots and garlic and fry for 5 minutes, until golden and tender. Add the sage leaves and some salt and pepper, then add the tomatoes and black olives. Pour in the white wine and bring to a boil. Boil for 2 minutes, then add the remaining oil, the lemon juice and a little salt. Simmer for 5 minutes, then remove from the heat and leave to cool to room temperature.

Either eat straight away or place the mixture in a large sterilized preserving jar and seal it. Place the jar in a large pan of cold water, bring slowly to a boil and simmer for 20 minutes. Remove and leave to cool. Store in a cool, dark place for up to 3 months.

PG TIPS You can vary the ingredients for this dish, using basil or oregano instead of sage, and vinegar instead of lemon juice.

'porcini, one of Italy's greatest treasures; highly prized for their wonderful earthy flavor'

Pan-fried Asparagus
with New-season Morels

1 lb. asparagus, trimmed (see
   page 170)
1/4 cup virgin olive oil
2 tablespoons unsalted butter
1/2 lb. fresh morel mushrooms,
   cleaned (see page 172)
3 garlic cloves, crushed
1 tablespoon chopped fresh parsley
1 tablespoon balsamic vinegar
Salt and coarsely ground black
   pepper

This is a simple recipe and I like to top it with a buttery fried egg.

Bring a large pot of salted water to a boil and add the asparagus. Blanch for 1 minute, then drain well.

Heat a tablespoon of the olive oil with half the butter in a large pan, add the asparagus and sauté until lightly golden, about 3–4 minutes. Remove the asparagus from the pan and keep warm. Heat the remaining oil and butter in the pan, add the morels and saute for 2–3 minutes. Add the garlic and sauté briefly. Finally stir in the parsley and balsamic vinegar. Season well, then cascade the morels over the asparagus and serve immediately.

PG TIPS If you cannot get fresh morels, replace them with 3 oz. mixed dried mushrooms, soaked in hot water for 30 minutes, then drained.

Fennel Pissaladière

1/4 cup virgin olive oil, plus a
   little extra for drizzling
2 garlic cloves, crushed
3/4 lb. fennel bulbs, fronds
   removed, very thinly sliced
A pinch of sugar
10 anchovy fillets, rinsed and drained
1 tablespoon black olives
1 teaspoon chopped fresh rosemary
Salt and freshly ground black pepper

For the dough:
1 teaspoon dried yeast
2/3 cup water
2 cups bread flour
1/2 teaspoon salt
1 tablespoon olive oil

Pissaladière is a Provençal version of pizza, normally made with onions and anchovies. My variation is made with fennel. Serve as a tempting starter or light lunch.

For the dough, dissolve the yeast in a little of the water. Sift the flour and salt into a bowl and make a well in the center. Pour the yeast liquid into the well with the remaining water and the olive oil and bring it all together with your hands to form a pliable dough. Knead on a lightly floured surface for 6–8 minutes, until smooth and elastic. Place the dough in a lightly oiled bowl, cover with a damp cloth, then leave at warm room temperature for 1 hour or until doubled in size.

Meanwhile, make the topping. Heat the oil in a pan, add the garlic and leave over a low heat to infuse for 5 minutes. Add the fennel and sugar, cover and sweat until the fennel is lightly caramelized and very tender.

Preheat the oven to 400°F. Punch down the dough and roll it out on a floured surface to a 10 x 8 in. rectangle. Place on a lightly oiled baking tray. Spread the fennel over the dough, garnish with the anchovy fillets and scatter over the olives and rosemary. Drizzle over a little olive oil and bake for 25–30 minutes or until the base is cooked through and slightly crusty.

'the arrival of
new-season
asparagus
and morels
heralds the
beginning of
Spring'

'a stunning
seafood
appetiser
to grace
any table'

Beefsteak Tomatoes
with Sardine and Fennel Risotto

2 tablespoons unsalted butter

1 small onion, finely chopped

1 garlic clove, crushed

1¼ cups vegetable or fish stock

⅔ cup arborio rice

1 fennel bulb, cut into ½ in. pieces

A good pinch of saffron strands

½ cup dry white wine

4 medium sardines, filleted and cut into small pieces

1 tablespoon chopped fresh dill

4 large, firm beefsteak tomatoes

1 tablespoon fresh white breadcrumbs

1 tablespoon freshly grated Parmesan cheese

Salt and freshly ground black pepper

Serve these stuffed tomatoes as an appetizer or as part of a summer lunch. I like to vary the fish from time to time depending on availability. Shrimp, mussels and tuna make good substitutes for the sardines.

Preheat the oven to 400°F. Melt the butter over a medium heat, add the onion and garlic and cook for 3–4 minutes. Heat the stock to simmering point in a separate pot. Add the rice, fennel and saffron to the onion and stir until the rice is coated with the butter. Add the wine and simmer until it has been absorbed by the rice. Then add a ladleful of the hot stock and cook, stirring, until it has almost all been absorbed. Keep adding stock in this way, stirring constantly, until the rice is just tender and all the liquid has been used up. Add the sardine fillets and dill a few minutes before the end of cooking and mix gently. Turn the risotto out on to a plate and leave to cool slightly, then season to taste.

Slice the tops off the tomatoes and scoop out the flesh and seeds. Dry the insides of the tomatoes carefully with paper towels, then season with salt and pepper. Fill generously with the risotto. Mix together the breadcrumbs and Parmesan and sprinkle them over the risotto.

Bake the tomatoes in the oven for 10–12 minutes, until they are tender but not overcooked. Serve hot from the oven, replacing the tops of the tomatoes, if liked. They are also good served cold.

PG TIPS Buy saffron strands rather than powder, if possible, as they have a much better flavor. However, both will give the risotto a deep yellowish-red tinge.

salad
leaves

Our salad bowls have been prettied up beyond all recognition over the last decade or so, thanks to the sudden surge of interest in green leaves. First to break the monopoly of the floppy butterhead lettuce was the iceberg, its crunch providing novel texture but little in the way of flavor. Better things followed thick and fast in the shape of unruly mops of frisée, handsome, russet oak-leaf lettuce, sweetly crisp romaine/cos and Little Gem, spicy, rugged mustard leaves, pretty but insipid corn salad and, the leaf that even salad haters find addictive, tender, spear-shaped arugula with its assertive peppery flavor. 'Green salad' is a bit of a misnomer nowadays, when it might equally well

Red chicory (left)

contain white-veined red radicchio or pale yellow endive.

Designer salad leaves command designer prices but many of the tastiest and most fashionable varieties can be grown surprisingly easily in the garden – Swiss chard, arugula and sorrel, for example.

Leafy vegetables are equally varied in flavor as appearance, ranging from the sweetness of more traditional varieties to the mouth-puckering astringency of sorrel and the bitterness of chicory and frisée. Balancing the tastes and textures of the leaves you include in your salad is almost as important as balancing your salad dressing. Although it's easy to open a bag of mixed salad where the choice has been made for you, it's much more fun to make up your own.

The interesting thing about all these newly popular salad greens is that they don't have to be confined to the salad bowl. Mature arugula is wonderful in soups, gratins and pasta sauces. Even lettuce can be braised or made into soup, while, for me, chicory and radicchio only come into their own when cooked, their bitter flavors taking on a much more complex edge when lightly caramelized or stewed slowly in butter. Conversely, many leafy vegetables we expect to eat cooked make interesting additions to salads when young and tender – a handful of tiny raw Swiss chard, spinach or sorrel leaves, for example, provides bite and freshness.

Arugula

Belgian endive (or white chicory

Mustardcress

Raddichio

Red chard

Red chicory

Romaine lettuce

Sorrel

Spinach

Swiss chard

Watercress

Fried Tomato and Mozzarella Sandwiches

2 firm beefsteak tomatoes
1 cow's milk mozzarella cheese
$^1/_2$ cup vegetable oil
1 garlic clove, crushed
10 fresh basil leaves, chopped
2 large eggs, beaten
$^1/_2$ cup all purpose flour
3 cups fresh white breadcrumbs
2 tablespoons unsalted butter
$^1/_2$ quantity of Anchoïade (see page 54)
Salt and freshly ground black pepper

Tomatoes, mozzarella and basil are a perfect marriage of ingredients, much loved by the Italians for years. These crisp, fried delicacies make a great appetizer, snack or light lunch.

Core the tomatoes and cut each one horizontally into 4 thick slices. Cut the mozzarella into 4 slices. Heat 2 tablespoons of the oil in a large frying pan until very hot. Add the tomato slices (in 2 batches if necessary) and sear without moving them until they are dark and almost caramelized, about 1 minute. Sprinkle the garlic and basil over the tomatoes. Turn them over carefully, sear on the other side, then season. Remove from the pan and leave to cool.

Meanwhile, beat the eggs in a bowl with 2 tablespoons of the remaining oil. Spread the flour out in a shallow dish and the breadcrumbs in another dish. Sandwich each slice of mozzarella between 2 tomato slices. Coat the sandwiches first in the flour, then in the beaten egg and finally in the breadcrumbs, patting them lightly to ensure they are well coated all over.

Heat the remaining vegetable oil and the butter in a large frying pan. When the butter begins to foam, add the sandwiches and cook until crisp and deep golden, about 2 minutes on each side. Remove with a spatula and drain on paper towels. Sprinkle with salt and serve on a small pool of the anchoïade.

PG TIPS When a recipe requires breadcrumbs, don't be tempted to buy those dry, sawdust-like grains that are good for nothing but the dustbin. Fresh breadcrumbs are easy to prepare: simply remove the crusts from slices of fresh white or brown bread and blitz in a food processor or blender until the crumbs are fine, soft and fluffy. They keep well in the freezer.

Twice-cooked Chestnut Mushrooms with Prosciutto and Taleggio

8 very large chestnut mushrooms
1/2 cup extra virgin olive oil
2/3 cup dry white wine
1 garlic clove, crushed
1 teaspoon chopped fresh rosemary
1/4 lb. prosciutto, cut into small
  dice (around 1 cup)
3 oz. Taleggio cheese, cut in
  1/4 in. dice (around 3/4 cup)
2 cups fresh white breadcrumbs
1 tablespoon freshly grated
  Parmesan cheese
Salt and freshly ground black pepper

Stuffed mushrooms appear in one guise or another in most restaurants, so here's one for the recipe album with all the flavors of Italy. Use extra virgin olive oil and the best prosciutto you can afford.

Preheat the oven to 350°F. Remove the stalks from the mushrooms and chop them roughly. Place the mushroom caps in an ovenproof dish, pour over 2 tablespoons of the olive oil and all the wine, then cover with foil and bake for 15 minutes.

Meanwhile, prepare the filling: heat another 2 tablespoons of the oil, add the garlic, rosemary and prosciutto and sauté for 4–5 minutes. Add the chopped mushroom stalks and cook for 2 minutes. Transfer to a bowl and leave to cool slightly. Add the Taleggio and breadcrumbs, season to taste and mix well.

Fill each mushroom with this mixture, then pour over the remaining oil and sprinkle with the grated Parmesan. Return to the oven and bake for 10 minutes, until bubbling and golden.

Bhurtho (Smoked Eggplant Dip)

2 eggplants
1/2 cup blanched almonds
1/2 teaspoon black mustard seeds
1/4 cup olive oil, plus extra to
  serve
1 onion, grated
1 chile, seeded and chopped
1 in. piece of fresh ginger,
  finely chopped
2 garlic cloves, crushed
Cayenne pepper, to taste
Juice of 1 lemon
2 tablespoons plain yoghurt
Salt
Chopped fresh coriander leaves, to
garnish

I just cannot get enough of this dip. It makes a great accompaniment to Asian-style dishes. Serve as a dip for raw vegetables or just on its own with lots of bread such as naan or parathas.

Prick the eggplants in several places with a small knife, then bake whole over a barbecue or in a hot oven for about an hour, until the skin is well charred and the flesh is soft when pierced with a knife. Leave to cool, then peel. Place the flesh in a deep bowl and mash it as finely as possible with a masher or a fork (do not use a food processor or blender).

Toast the almonds and mustard seeds in a dry frying pan for 1–2 minutes, then add the olive oil, onion, chile and ginger and cook for a further 5 minutes over a low heat. Transfer to a small blender and blend to a purée.

Add the almond mixture to the mashed aubergine and mix in the garlic, cayenne pepper and some salt. Add the lemon juice and yoghurt. Transfer to a serving bowl and, with the back of a hot spoon, make a hollow in the center. Pour in a little olive oil and sprinkle with some chopped coriander leaves.

Caponata 'Mildly Moroccan'

2 medium eggplants

2 red peppers

3 tablespoons olive oil

1 small onion, finely chopped

2 celery stalks, finely diced

3 tablespoons maple syrup

2 tablespoons red wine vinegar

1 lb. tomatoes, skinned,
    seeded and chopped

12 green olives

2 tablespoons pine nuts, toasted

Salt and freshly ground black pepper

For the Moroccan spice mix:

1/2 teaspoon each ground cumin,
    coriander and paprika

1 tablespoon chopped coriander
    leaves

A fusion dish from the Mediterranean rim, taking the best from Italy and Morocco to form a wonderful blend of flavors. All you need is lots of good bread to mop up the juices.

Cut the eggplants and peppers into ¾-inch dice. Heat the olive oil in a large pan, add the onion and celery and sauté until lightly golden. Add the eggplant and peppers, reduce the heat and cook until the vegetables begin to soften, about 10 minutes. Combine all the ingredients for the spice mix, add to the vegetables and cook for 5 minutes. Stir in the maple syrup and vinegar, then the tomatoes and olives. Cook, uncovered, for 30–40 minutes, until the vegetables are tender. Season to taste and serve warm or cold, topped with the toasted pine nuts.

PG TIPS Replace the fresh tomatoes with 14 oz. chopped canned tomatoes, if need be.

Okra Fritters with Chickpea Almond Tarator

2 garlic cloves, crushed

1/2 teaspoon salt

2/3 cup cooked chickpeas, puréed

5 tablespoons tahini

2/3 cup ground almonds

1/2 cup light olive oil

3 tablespoons lemon juice

2 tablespoons chopped coriander
    leaves

For the batter:

1 cup besan flour (gram)

1/2 teaspoon baking soda

1/2 teaspoon ground cumin

1/2 teaspoon ground coriander

1/4 teaspoon ground turmeric

1 small green chile, seeded and
    finely chopped

Salt and freshly ground black pepper

Vegetable oil for deep-frying

3/4 lb. okra, trimmed

For the tarator, put the garlic and salt in a bowl and blend to a paste. Beat in the puréed chickpeas, tahini and ground almonds, then drizzle in the olive oil and lemon juice, stirring constantly. Add a little water to bring it to a dipping consistency and stir in the fresh coriander leaves.

Sift together the gram flour, baking soda and spices, then stir in the chile. Beat in enough warm water to form a batter that coats the back of a spoon. Season with salt and pepper.

Heat some oil in a deep pot or deep-fat fryer to about 350°F. Dip the okra in the batter and fry in batches for about 4–5 minutes or until golden. Drain well on paper towels, sprinkle with coarse salt and serve with the tarator.

'crisp and
exotically
spiced
fritters with
a smooth
almond sauce'

Spinach, Chile and Black Bean Fritters

1¹/₄ cups milk

²/₃ stick (¹/₄ cup, plus 1 tablespoon) unsalted butter

1 cup besan flour (gram /)

3 eggs

¹/₂ cup freshly cooked spinach, roughly chopped

2 tablespoons chopped fresh coriander leaves

³/₄ cup cooked black beans, roughly chopped

¹/₂ in. piece of fresh ginger, finely grated

1 teaspoon chopped seeded green chile

1 teaspoon cumin seeds

¹/₂ teaspoon fenugreek seeds

¹/₂ teaspoon mustard seeds

1 teaspoon lemon juice

Vegetable oil for frying

Salt

To serve:

¹/₂ cup Green Tomato and Pepper Chutney (see page 148)

¹/₂ cup plain yoghurt

Crisp, spicy fritters that every vegetarian will love.

Put the milk and butter in a pan and heat until the butter has melted and the milk is coming to a boil, then rain in the flour. Beat until it becomes a smooth paste, then cook for a few minutes over a low heat. Spoon the mixture into a large bowl and leave to cool for 5 minutes before beating in the eggs one at a time. Add the spinach, coriander leaves, black beans, ginger, chile and the cumin, fenugreek and mustard seeds, then season with a little salt. Add the lemon juice and adjust the seasoning if necessary.

Pour some vegetable oil into a pan to a depth of about 4 inches and heat. Drop in the mixture in small spoonfuls and fry until golden; remove them from the oil when they start to burst. Drain on paper towels, then arrange on serving plates. Garnish with the chutney and pour the yoghurt around, then serve immediately.

PG TIPS To cook spinach, wash it well, then put it in a pan with just the water clinging to its leaves. Cover with a tight-fitting lid and cook very gently for a few minutes until wilted. Drain very well and stir in a little butter, salt, pepper and nutmeg.

Cardoon Fritters
with Parmesan Caper Aïoli

1¹/₂ lbs. cardoons
Juice of 2 lemons
1 small onion, grated
¹/₂ garlic clove, crushed
¹/₂ cup vegetable oil, plus
   extra for deep-frying
1 quantity of Herb Aïoli (see page
   85)
1 tablespoon freshly grated
   Parmesan cheese
2 tablespoons superfine capers, well
   drained
Salt
Lemon quarters, to serve

For the batter:
1¹/₄ cups all purpose flour
1¹/₂ teaspoons salt
1 teaspoon grated lemon zest
2 eggs
3 tablespoons olive oil
Juice of 1 lemon
³/₄ cup beer, at room
   temperature

Cardoons are popular in Italy and France but unfortunately not so much in the UK. The inner stalks and roots are very pleasant served like asparagus and also make excellent fritters. Celery would be a suitable alternative.

Trim the cardoons (see page 170), rub with a little of the lemon juice and cut into 4-inch lengths. Bring a large pot of water to a boil, add the juice of 1 lemon and some salt, then add the cardoons and cook for 15–20 minutes, until just tender. Remove and drain well.

Mix together the onion, garlic, vegetable oil and remaining lemon juice, add the hot cardoons and leave to marinate for 1 hour. Then remove from the marinade and dry thoroughly on paper towels.

To prepare the batter, sift the flour and salt into a bowl and add the lemon zest. Make a well in the center, add the eggs and beat until blended. Add the oil, lemon juice and beer, whisk well together, then cover and leave to rest for 1 hour at room temperature. Meanwhile, mix together the aïoli, Parmesan and capers.

Heat some oil for deep-frying to 325°F. Dip the cardoons in the batter and fry until golden brown. Drain on paper towels, then serve immediately with the lemon quarters and aïoli.

PG TIPS When preparing a flour-based batter, always allow it to rest before using. This gives the flour time to work, making the end result more homogeneous.

Celeriac Waffles with Smoked Salmon,
Horseradish Cream and Caviar

3/4 lb. celeriac
2 1/2 cups whole milk, boiled
2 eggs
1 egg yolk
6 tablespoons all purpose flour
1 tablespoon heavy cream
Freshly grated nutmeg
2 tablespoons unsalted butter
**7 oz. smoked salmon, thinly
  sliced**
1 tablespoon caviar
Salt and freshly ground black pepper

For the horseradish cream:
**5 tablespoons heavy cream,
  semi-whipped**
1 tablespoon snipped fresh chives
**1 tablespoon finely grated fresh
  horseradish**
1 teaspoon lemon juice

I first cooked vegetable waffles when I worked in Paris. They were made of potato blended with shredded vegetables and were used to garnish game dishes. Since those days I have experimented with all manner of vegetables. Corn and squash have been successful, as has this combination of celeriac and smoked salmon.

Peel the celeriac and cut it into chunks, then cook in the boiled milk for 20–25 minutes until tender. Drain well, reserving the milk. Pass the celeriac through a sieve or mash until smooth. Put it in a bowl with the eggs and egg yolk, flour, 2/3 cup of the cooking milk and the cream. Mix well, season with salt, pepper and nutmeg and leave to rest for an hour. Meanwhile, make the horseradish cream: carefully fold together the cream, chives and horseradish, season to taste, then stir in the lemon juice.

Heat a waffle maker until almost smoking and then add a quarter of the butter to each waffle compartment. Pour in a small ladleful of the mixture, close the lid and cook as for normal waffles.
Place a good spoonful of horseradish cream on each warm waffle and top with the smoked salmon and caviar. Serve immediately.

Celery Anchoïade

1 large head of celery
**Ciabatta or other rustic country
  bread, to serve**

For the anchoïade:
3/4 stick (1/3 cup) unsalted butter
6 tablespoons virgin olive oil
2 garlic cloves, very finely chopped
1 teaspoon fresh thyme
2 tablespoons chopped fresh basil
**3 oz. anchovy fillets, drained and
  finely chopped (around 1/3 cup)**
1 tablespoon white wine vinegar
1 teaspoon Dijon mustard
Salt and freshly ground black pepper

This is a play on the Provençal speciality of raw vegetables with a warm garlic and anchovy dipping sauce. The anchoïade keeps well in a sealed jar in the refrigerator and can be reheated gently before use.

Trim the celery and peel each stalk with a vegetable peeler to remove its stringy fibers. Cut into 2-inch lengths and cook in a pan of lightly salted boiling water for 10 minutes. Drain and leave to cool.

For the sauce, melt the butter and olive oil in a pan, add the garlic and herbs and cook for 1 minute, until fragrant. Add the anchovies and cook over a gentle heat for 8–10 minutes, stirring occasionally. Season lightly, then whisk in the vinegar and mustard.

Arrange the celery on a serving dish and pour over the warm anchovy and garlic sauce. Serve with chunks of rustic bread to mop up those wonderful garlicky juices.

'a waffle with a difference - the perfect partner for smoked salmon and caviar'

chapter **two**

main
courses

In this chapter you will find some substantial dishes to serve as a centerpiece for a meal - the Turnip, Cabbage and Mustard Torte on page 74, for instance, or the Okra, Spinach and Chickpea Tagine on page 59. But there are also plenty of lighter choices, such as Spring Risotto (page 60) or Minted Shallot Custard Tart (page 58), inspired by new-season's vegetables and ideal for warmer days. Although some people prefer to stick to a traditional meal structure it's just as acceptable now to serve a collection of little dishes - something that works especially well with vegetable cookery - so do look through the other chapters in this book for ideas. When deciding what goes with what, I find it best to think geographically - choosing a selection of Mediterranean dishes, for example, or those with an Asian influence.

Minted Shallot Custard Tart

½ stick (¼ cup) unsalted butter

1 lb. banana shallots, thinly
   sliced (see page 67)

1 teaspoon sugar

Freshly grated nutmeg

5 tablespoons dry sherry

2 eggs

2 egg yolks

1¼ cups heavy cream

a scant cup milk

1 tablespoon chopped fresh mint

Salt and freshly ground black pepper

For the pastry dough:

2¼ cups all purpose flour

1½ sticks (¾ cup) chilled unsalted
   butter, cut into small pieces

1 egg, beaten

A pinch of salt

For the pastry dough, sift the flour on to a work surface or into a large bowl. Add the butter and blend together with your fingertips until it has a soft, sandy texture. Make a well in the center and add the beaten egg and salt. Gently mix together with your fingertips to form a smooth, even dough. Wrap in plastic wrap and chill for about 30 minutes.

Preheat the oven to 375°F. Roll out the dough and use to line a 9-inch quiche pan. Line with wax paper, fill with baking beans and bake blind for 8–10 minutes. Remove the paper and beans and return the pastry to the oven for 5 minutes, then leave to cool.

Heat the butter in a frying pan, add the shallots, then sprinkle the sugar over and season with salt, pepper and nutmeg. Turn the shallots and cook for 5–8 minutes, until lightly caramelized. Add the sherry, cover the pan and cook for about 20 minutes, until the shallots are tender. Drain and leave to cool.

For the custard, beat the eggs, yolks, cream and milk together until well amalgamated. Stir in the mint and some salt, pepper and nutmeg. Arrange the shallots in the pie crust and pour on the custard. Bake for 30–35 minutes or until just set. Serve warm.

Tian of Tomato, Zucchini and Fennel
with Roquefort

6 tablespoons olive oil

1 onion, thinly sliced

1 garlic clove, crushed

¾ lb. fennel, thinly sliced

1 lb. small zucchini, sliced

1 lb. ripe but firm tomatoes,
   sliced

½ tablespoon summer savory

½ tablespoon fresh thyme

½ lb. Roquefort cheese,
   crumbled (around 2 cups)

2 tablespoons fresh white
   breadcrumbs

Salt and freshly ground black pepper

A tian is a Provençal earthenware dish suitable for all manner of gratins. Any large, shallow baking dish would be fine.

Preheat the oven to 350°F. Heat 3 tablespoons of the oil in a pan, add the onion, garlic and fennel and cook over a moderate heat for about 10–15 minutes, until lightly golden and tender. Season well. Place the mixture in a baking dish, then arrange the zucchini and tomatoes on top, overlapping in rows. Sprinkle with salt, pepper and the savory and thyme. Sprinkle with 2 tablespoons of the remaining olive oil and bake for 30–35 minutes. Remove from the oven, sprinkle with the Roquefort, breadcrumbs and remaining oil and return to the oven for 10 minutes, then serve.

PG TIPS To grate or crumble soft cheese, freeze it for up to one hour. It will then grate or crumble much more easily and will not stick to the grater and become messy.

Okra, Spinach and Sweet Potato Tagine with Chermoula Couscous Fritters

2 tablespoons olive oil

1 red onion, chopped

2 garlic cloves, crushed

1 teaspoon ground coriander

1/2 teaspoon ground cumin

3/4 lb. orange-fleshed sweet potatoes, peeled and cut into chunks

1 1/2 teaspoons harissa

1 tablespoon tomato paste

3/4 lb. small okra, trimmed

14 oz. canned chopped tomatoes, drained

2 cups chicken or vegetable stock

3 tablespoons chopped fresh coriander leaves, plus extra to garnish

5 oz. fresh spinach, washed (around 2-3 large handfuls)

Salt and freshly ground black pepper

For the fritters:

1/3 cup couscous

1/2 cup hot water

1 oz. fresh coriander leaves (around a handful)

1 small garlic clove, chopped

3 tablespoons olive oil

1/2 teaspoon ground cumin

1/2 teaspoon ground coriander

2 tablespoons pine nuts, toasted

2 oz. feta cheese, finely diced (around a 1/2 cup)

2 medium eggs, beaten

3 cups fine white breadcrumbs (see Tips on page 48)

2 tablespoons all purpose flour

Vegetable oil for deep-frying

A tagine is a type of Moroccan stew, made with meat, fish or vegetables and named after the earthenware pot it is cooked in. This vegetarian version is spiced with harissa, a hot condiment that adds real zest to dishes.

Heat the oil in a large pot, add the onion, garlic, ground coriander, cumin and sweet potatoes and cook for 5 minutes over a moderate heat until just beginning to brown. Add the harissa and tomato paste and cook for 2 minutes. Add the okra, stir well and cook for a further 2 minutes, then stir in the chopped tomatoes, stock and fresh coriander leaves. Bring to a boil, reduce the heat and simmer gently for 10–15 minutes or until the okra is tender and the sauce has thickened. Add the spinach and cook for a further 2 minutes. Season with salt and pepper.

For the fritters, place the couscous in a large bowl and pour over the hot water. Leave to soak for 10 minutes, until all the water has been absorbed, and then fluff up with a fork. Place the coriander leaves and garlic in a small blender with the olive oil and spices and blend to a thick purée. Add to the couscous, along with the toasted pine nuts and feta. Season to taste and bind with half the beaten egg and half the breadcrumbs to form a firm mixture. Shape into 12 small balls. Dip each one into the flour, then into the remaining beaten egg, and finally into the remaining breadcrumbs, ensuring that they are evenly coated.

Heat some oil for deep-frying until it is hot enough for a small cube of bread to turn golden in 1 minute. Add the fritters a few at a time and fry for 3 minutes, until crisp and golden. Drain on paper towels and keep warm while you fry the rest.

Serve the tagine with the couscous fritters, garnished with fresh coriander leaves.

PG TIPS Some boiled plain or saffron-flavored rice would also make a good accompaniment to the tagine, instead of the fritters.

Southern-style Okra Succotash

4 corn on the cob, husks removed
1/2 stick (1/4 cup) unsalted butter
3/4 lb. small okra, trimmed
4 scallions, shredded
1/2 red pepper, cut into small dice
1/2 green pepper, cut into small dice
1/2 garlic clove, crushed
1/2 teaspoon dried thyme
1/2 teaspoon ground paprika
1/2 teaspoon ground cumin
14 oz. can of lima beans
1 1/2 teaspoons lemon juice
Salt and freshly ground black pepper

A favorite in the Deep South, succotash is a stew of corn, lima beans and, sometimes, peppers. My version includes okra (also known as ladies fingers in the UK), another popular ingredient in the South, and is pepped up with some delicate spices. The name succotash is taken from the Narragansett Indian word misickquatash, meaning boiled whole corn kernels.

Using a small knife, cut off the corn kernels, letting them drop into a bowl along with any juices from the corn.

Dice half the butter and chill it. Heat the remaining butter in a large frying pan, add the okra, scallions and peppers and cook over a moderate heat for 3–4 minutes. Add the corn, garlic, thyme and spices, lower the heat and cook until fragrant, about 4–5 minutes. Add the canned beans and their liquid, stirring them in to heat through. Season to taste, stir in the lemon juice and then whisk in the reserved butter a few pieces at a time.

Spring Risotto

1 stick (1/2 cup) unsalted butter
2 shallots, finely chopped
1 quart vegetable or
   chicken stock
5 oz. fresh morels, cleaned
   (see page 72) or 2 oz. dried
   morels, soaked in hot water for 30
   minutes, then drained
1 1/3 cups arborio rice
1/3 cup dry white wine
3/4 lb. fresh peas (shelled
   weight)
2 tablespoons freshly grated
   Parmesan cheese
1 tablespoon chopped fresh mint
2 oz. pea shoots/young pea
   tendrils (optional)
Salt and freshly ground black pepper

The beginning of the British summer is heralded by the arrival of tender new peas. This is one of my favorite ways to use them, in a smooth, creamy purée that binds the delicate rice grains. The morels add an earthy quality to the dish.

Melt half the butter in a large, heavy-based pan, add the shallots and cook gently until tender. In a separate pot, heat the stock to simmering point. Add the morels to the shallots and cook for 1 minute. Add the rice and stir well to coat it with the butter, then pour in the wine and bring to a boil. Add a ladleful of the stock and cook, stirring, over a low-to-medium heat, until it has all been absorbed by the rice. Keep adding the stock a ladleful at a time, stirring constantly, until the rice is tender but still retains a little bite – it should take about 25 minutes in all.

Meanwhile cook the peas in plenty of boiling salted water until tender. Drain them well, then place half of them in a blender and blitz to a smooth purée.

When the risotto is ready, it should be fairly coarse in consistency without being sloppy. Add the pea purée to the rice and season to taste, then add the cooked peas. Finally fork in the Parmesan, the remaining butter and the mint. Divide between 4 serving plates, sprinkle over the pea shoots, if using, and serve immediately.

'okra adds another dimension to a southern-style vegetable favorite'

Claypot-baked Roots
with Mustard Baste

4 small carrots, peeled but left whole

1 small rutabaga, peeled and cut into
wedges

6 small parsnips, peeled but left
whole

1 turnip, peeled and cut into wedges

2 red onions, peeled and cut into
wedges through the root

1 celeriac, peeled and cut into
wedges

2 salsify, peeled and cut into 1 in.
lengths

2/3 cup dry white wine

1 teaspoon coriander seeds

For the baste:

1 1/2 teaspoons Dijon mustard

1/4 cup olive oil

1 garlic clove, crushed

1 teaspoon mixed dried herbs

Salt and freshly ground black pepper

Clay cooking pots became popular in the Seventies and quite a few people have one tucked away in a kitchen cupboard. It is important to soak them before use so that they do not crack in the heat of the oven.

Place all the ingredients for the baste in a large bowl and mix well. Add the vegetables, cover and leave to marinate for several hours, preferably overnight.

The next day, soak a claypot in cold water for 2 hours, then dry. Preheat the oven to 450°F. Put the vegetables and marinade in the claypot and bake for 30–35 minutes, until golden and slightly caramelized. Add the wine and coriander seeds and bake for a further 15 minutes so that the vegetables steam in the wine.

Remove the dish from the oven, carefully toss the vegetables and serve from the pot.

PG TIPS Some chefs would not work without a garlic press. I personally find that they work with frustrating irregularity and end up gathering dust at the back of my kitchen drawer. I prefer to crush garlic by simply peeling it, chopping it finely with a little salt, then using the flat of the knife blade to crush it to a smooth paste.

Colombo Chow-chow

2 tablespoons vegetable oil

1 lb. chayote (chow-chow), peeled, cored, seeded and cut into large chunks

1 onion, chopped

1 teaspoon cardamom pods, crushed, black seeds removed

1 in. piece of fresh ginger, grated

1 garlic clove, crushed

2 red chiles, seeded and chopped

1 teaspoon fennel seeds

1 teaspoon colombo curry powder (or any mild curry powder)

14 oz. can of unsweetened coconut milk

2/3 cup chicken or vegetable stock

2 fresh curry leaves

1 teaspoon ground turmeric

Salt and freshly ground black pepper

Fresh coriander leaves, to garnish

Colombo is a general term for curry in the Caribbean. Colombo powder is a type of curry powder that is usually mild but fragrant.

Heat the oil in a large pot, add the chayote, onion, cardamom seeds and ginger and cook for 2–3 minutes. Add the garlic, chiles, fennel seeds and curry powder and cook over a low heat until the vegetables begin to soften. Stir in the coconut milk, stock, curry leaves and turmeric, bring to a boil and cook over a low heat for 10–15 minutes or until the chayote is tender and the sauce has reduced and thickened slightly. Season to taste, then transfer to a serving dish and sprinkle with coriander leaves. Serve with fragrant rice.

PG TIPS Chow-chow, or chayote, is a very versatile vegetable and in the Caribbean it is even used in desserts. In one of my favorites it is flambéed with rum and dark brown sugar until caramelized, then served with coconut ice cream.

Thai Coconut-scented Eggplant
with Nam Pla

1/2 cup vegetable oil

1 lb. Japanese eggplants,
   sliced into rounds 1/2-inch thick

2 garlic cloves, crushed

1/2 teaspoon grated fresh ginger

1 1/2 teaspoons rice wine vinegar

1 tablespoon Asian chili sauce

2 tablespoons nam pla (Thai fish
   sauce)

14 oz. can of unsweetened
   coconut milk

Juice of 1 lime

A pinch of sugar

4 scallions, finely shredded

Salt

Heat the oil in a large frying pan or wok until very hot, then add the eggplant and stir-fry until tender – about 5–6 minutes. Drain the oil from the eggplant and place on paper towels to mop up any excess.

Heat 2 tablespoons of the drained oil in a pot, add the garlic, ginger and vinegar and stir, then add the chili sauce, fish sauce and coconut milk. Bring to a boil, add the eggplant to the sauce and cook over a moderate heat for about 10–12 minutes.

Stir in the lime juice, sugar and salt. Arrange over rice in a serving dish, sprinkle over it the scallions, and serve.

PG TIPS Coconut milk is much more commonplace than it used to be but I still find it an exciting ingredient. When it is cooked with fragrant spices and herbs its flavor is enhanced beyond recognition. Always be sure to check the label when purchasing coconut milk; it is very frustrating to get home to find you have picked up the sweet variety – I talk from experience!

'a melange
of mild Thai
flavors
boosted
with a little
chili sauce'

Wood Blewit Omelette

Serves 1

1 tablespoon virgin olive oil

1 shallot, finely chopped

3 oz. wood blewit mushrooms,
cleaned (see page 72) and thickly
sliced

A little lemon juice

1/2 stick (1/4 cup) unsalted butter

3 eggs

1/4 cup heavy cream

2 tablespoons fresh flat-leaf parsley
leaves

Salt and freshly ground black pepper

Wood blewits, more commonly known just as blewits, are very well-flavored mushrooms, ideal for pickling, soups or omelettes. The large caps are also good brushed with olive oil and broiled, then doused with soy sauce and sprinkled with herbs. If you cannot obtain wood blewits, you could substitute girolles, porcini or chanterelles. Serve this omelette with a crisp green salad and some sautéed potatoes.

Preheat the oven to 400°F. Heat the oil in a frying pan until very hot, add the shallot and blewits and sauté quickly for 5 minutes. Add 1/4 cup of water and continue to cook until the mushrooms are soft. Add the lemon juice, season to taste and remove from the heat.

Heat the butter in a heavy-based omelette pan with an ovenproof handle. Meanwhile, beat the eggs and cream together in a bowl with 1/4 cup of water, then season well and add the parsley. Pour the egg mixture into the omelette pan and add the blewits.

Cook for 30 seconds, lifting the cooked edges of the omelette to allow the uncooked egg to flow underneath. The omelette should remain runny in the center. Fold the omelette over, then place the pan in the oven for 2 minutes or until the omelette is puffed and golden.

PG TIPS If you don't have an ovenproof omelette pan, slide the folded omelette on to a baking tray before transferring it to the oven.

Baked Banana Shallots Stuffed with Red Chard and Basmati

12 large banana shallots

1/2 stick (1/4 cup) unsalted butter

1 garlic clove, crushed

1 cup button mushrooms,
chopped

5 oz. red chard (leaves and stalks),
finely chopped (around 2 1/3 cups)

3/4 cup basmati rice, cooked

3 tablespoons grated Gruyère or
Swiss cheese

1 tablespoon fresh thyme

1 tablespoon virgin olive oil

Salt and freshly ground black pepper

So-called because of their shape, banana shallots are larger and stronger-flavored than ordinary ones. They are particularly suitable for stuffing – here with a mixture of red chard and my favorite rice, the nutty-flavored basmati. This dish makes a good vegetarian main course. I like to serve it with spinach lightly bound with cream or with other green vegetables such as broccoli or green beans.

Preheat the oven to 400°F. Trim off the tops and roots of the shallots and peel them. Blanch in boiling water for 5 minutes, then drain well and leave to cool. Cut in half and, using a melon baller, scoop out a hollow in each shallot half.

Chop the scooped-out shallot flesh and fry in the butter with the garlic and mushrooms until tender and golden. Add the chard and sweat for 10 minutes, then transfer to a bowl and leave to cool. Add the rice, grated cheese and thyme and season to taste.

Stuff the shallots with the rice mixture, then place in an ovenproof dish, drizzle with the oil and cover with foil. Bake for 15–20 minutes, then remove the foil and bake for a further 10 minutes or until golden. Serve immediately.

PG TIPS To cook perfect rice, place in a large bowl and wash with cold running water until the water runs clear. Leave to soak in cold water for 30 minutes, then drain well. Place in a heavy-based pot, add a little salt and level the rice, then add just enough water to cover the rice by about 1 inch. Bring to a boil, cover with a tight-fitting lid and reduce the heat to very low. Leave undisturbed for about 20 minutes, then check that all the liquid has been absorbed. Fluff up the rice with a fork; this helps separate the grains and release the trapped steam.

Baked Eggplant with Samfaina

**5 squat, plump eggplants, stalks
  removed**
¹/₂ cup olive oil
2 red peppers
1 onion, finely chopped
1 garlic clove, crushed
1 teaspoon ground cumin
¹/₂ teaspoon hot smoked paprika
2 anchovy fillets, finely chopped
**8 fresh basil leaves, chopped, plus 4
  sprigs of basil to garnish**
1 tablespoon chopped fresh parsley
**3 oz. manchego (or Cheddar)
  cheese, coarsely grated (around
  ³/₄ cup)**
Salt and freshly ground black pepper

Samfaina is a type of Spanish ratatouille. I was introduced to this variation on it by Peter Doyle of the Cicada restaurant in Sydney, during a promotion at the Lanesborough. The flavors are wonderfully intense, whether it is served hot or cold. The better the smoked paprika is, the better the dish will taste. Smoked paprika is becoming popular in restaurants and can be found in good delicatessens. It is well worth tracking down.

Preheat the oven to 400°F. Rub the eggplants with half of the olive oil and then prick them all over with a small knife. Wrap them in foil so they are totally enclosed, place on a baking sheet and bake for 15–20 minutes. Rub the red peppers with 2 tablespoons of the oil, put them on the baking sheet and roast for about 25 minutes, until charred and soft. Remove the eggplants from the foil and leave until cool enough to handle. Slice a lid from the top (the stalk end) of 4 of the eggplants and scoop out the flesh, being careful not to split the skin. Finely chop the scooped-out flesh and the remaining whole eggplant.

Heat the remaining oil in a pan, add the onion and garlic, then cover and sweat for 10–15 minutes, until soft and pale golden. Meanwhile, peel and seed the roasted peppers and chop finely. Add to the onion, then stir in the cumin and paprika and cook for 5 minutes. Add the chopped eggplant, anchovies and herbs and cook for 2 minutes. Season to taste with salt and pepper.

Fill each eggplant with the samfaina, sprinkle the cheese over them and return to the oven for about 5 minutes, until bubbly and golden. Garnish with the basil sprigs and serve.

'oven-roasted eggplant with a deep and smoky center'

Parsnip Gnocchi with Girolles, Trompettes and Sour Cherries

3 lbs. parsnips, cut into small
   chunks
2 tablespoons vegetable oil
³/₄ cup water
1 stick (¹/₂ cup) unsalted butter
1 cup, plus 2 tablespoons all purpose
   flour
4 eggs
8 small fresh sage leaves
5 oz. mixed girolles and
   trompettes (or other mixed wild
   mushrooms), cleaned (see page
   172)
¹/₂ cup dried sour cherries
¹/₄ cup tamari
²/₃ cup vegetable stock
Salt and freshly ground black pepper

In my kitchen I treat parsnips with the respect I would give asparagus or artichokes. When they are roasted in butter their wonderful sweet flavor has no rival. They are also good used in soups and stews to give an earthy flavor. Here I've used them to make gnocchi, with wild mushrooms to add a little touch of luxury. Trompettes can be hard to find but almost any other type of mushroom can be substituted.

Preheat the oven to 400°F. Blanch the parsnips in a large pot of boiling water for 2 minutes, then drain well. Transfer to a baking sheet, spoon over them the oil, and roast for about 30 minutes, until lightly golden. Purée in a blender or food processor.

Put the water, half the butter and a pinch of salt in a pan and heat until the butter melts and the water comes to a boil. Rain in the flour, stirring vigorously until the mixture forms a mass and leaves the side of the pan clean – about 2–3 minutes. Transfer to a large bowl and then beat in the eggs one at a time. Beat in the parsnip purée and season to taste.

Spoon large spoonfuls of the mixture on to a greased baking sheet, leaving at least 2 inches between each spoonful. Bake for about 20–25 minutes, until crisp and beginning to brown.

Heat the remaining butter in a frying pan, add the sage leaves and leave to infuse for 1 minute. Add the mushrooms and sauté for 1 minute, then add the cherries and tamari. Pour the vegetable stock in and boil for 3 minutes, until the sauce thickens. Season to taste. Pour the sauce on to serving plates and top with the gnocchi. Serve immediately.

Fava Bean, Potato and Ricotta Polpettone with Salsa Verde

1 lb., 5 oz. floury potatoes, such
    as Russet
3 tablespoons ricotta cheese
1 cup freshly grated Parmesan
    cheese
2²/₃ cups fresh white breadcrumbs
2 egg yolks
Freshly grated nutmeg
¹/₂ stick (¹/₄ cup) unsalted butter
3 oz. chestnut mushrooms,
    chopped (around ³/₄ cup)
1 garlic clove, crushed
¹/₄ lb. fava beans, cooked (around ¹/₂
    cup) dried, pre-soaked fava beans
    would also be suitable
1 tablespoon chopped fresh oregano
1 tablespoon chopped fresh parsley
Flour for dusting
2 eggs, beaten
¹/₄ cup olive oil
Salt and freshly ground black pepper

For the salsa verde:
¹/₂ cup fresh parsley (leaves only)
¹/₄ cup fresh mint (leaves only)
1 teaspoon superfine capers, drained
1 teaspoon Dijon mustard
2 garlic cloves, peeled
1 teaspoon white wine vinegar
¹/₄ cup virgin olive oil

Polpettone is the Italian term for a type of rissole, usually made with vegetables, coated in egg and breadcrumbs, then fried.

For the salsa verde, put all the ingredients in a blender or food processor and blitz to a coarse purée. Set aside.

Cook the unpeeled potatoes in boiling salted water until tender, then drain well. Leave to cool slightly before peeling them. Push the peeled potatoes through a vegetable mill or strainer. Place in a large bowl with the ricotta, Parmesan and half the breadcrumbs, then bind with the egg yolks. Season well with salt, pepper and nutmeg and chill for about 30 minutes.

Meanwhile, heat 1 tablespoon of the butter in a frying pan, add the mushrooms and garlic and sauté over a high heat until golden. Stir in the fava beans, oregano and parsley, season to taste and remove from the heat. Leave to cool.

Divide the potato mixture into quarters and shape each one into a ball. Dust your hands with flour and, holding a potato ball in the palm of one hand, make an indentation in the center and fill with the mushroom mixture. Reshape the potato round it so the filling is completely enclosed. Flatten into a pattie shape, ensuring the filling stays well sealed. Prepare the other 3 portions in the same way.

Put the remaining breadcrumbs in a shallow dish. Put the beaten eggs in a separate dish. Dip the polpettone first in the beaten egg and then in the breadcrumbs, pressing them on to coat. Heat the remaining butter in a frying pan with the olive oil and fry the polpettone until golden, 3–5 minutes on each side. Arrange the polpettone on a serving dish, pour over a little of the salsa verde and serve.

Golden Zucchini and Shrimp Couscous
with Preserved Lemon and Olives

1²/3 cups couscous

2¹/4 cups boiling water

2 tablespoons light olive oil

16 large raw shrimp, deveined

1 red chile, seeded and finely
  chopped

1 garlic clove, crushed

4 small golden zucchini, sliced

2 tablespoons flaked almonds,
  toasted

3 tablespoons golden raisins

12 black olives

2 tablespoons chopped fresh mint

1 teaspoon chopped preserved
  salted lemon

Salt and freshly ground black pepper

For the dressing:

1/2 cup olive oil

Juice of 1 lemon

1 garlic clove, crushed

1 tablespoon white wine vinegar

1 tablespoon chopped fresh mint

Inspired by Moroccan flavors, this is a vibrant array of colors and aromas. Chicken or salmon could be used instead of the shrimp.

Place the couscous in a large bowl, pour the boiling water over it, then cover and leave for 5 minutes. Fluff up the couscous with a fork, then cover again and leave for 5 minutes longer. Fluff up again and season to taste.

Heat the oil in a frying pan, add the shrimp, chile, garlic and zucchini and sauté for 3–4 minutes, until the shrimp and zucchini are cooked. Add the toasted almonds, raisins, olives, mint and preserved lemon, then season to taste. Add to the couscous and toss well together.

Whisk all the ingredients for the dressing together and season to taste. Toss with the couscous and serve warm.

PG TIPS Preserved salted lemons are popular throughout the Mediterranean and the Middle East. You can buy them in some large supermarkets and delicatessens.

'spicy
shrimp and
couscous –
a flavor
sensation'

Turnip, Cabbage and Mustard Torte

Serves 6

¹/₂ Savoy cabbage, core removed, thinly sliced

1 lb., 5 oz. medium turnips, peeled and cut into slices ¹/₈-inch thick

¹/₂ stick (¹/₄ cup) unsalted butter, melted

¹/₄ cup vegetable oil

2 onions, thinly sliced

1 teaspoon cumin seeds

1¹/₂ teaspoons Dijon mustard

1¹/₄ cups grated Cheddar cheese

¹/₂ cup crème fraîche or sour cream

Salt and freshly ground black pepper

A delicious rustic layered cake of winter vegetables spiked with Dijon mustard. Serve as a vegetarian main course or as an accompaniment to meat dishes.

Preheat the oven to 400°F. Cook the cabbage in boiling salted water for about 3 minutes, until just tender, then drain, refresh under cold running water and dry well.

Place the turnip slices in a bowl and mix with the melted butter and some salt and pepper.

Heat the oil in a pan, add the onions and cumin seeds and fry for about 8 minutes or until golden. Season to taste and then place in a bowl to cool. When cold, mix in the mustard and set aside.

Take a deep baking dish 8–10 inches in diameter and arrange about a third of the turnips over the bottom. Cover with a layer of Cheddar (save ¹/₄ cup for the topping), then a third of the cabbage, then a third of the onions. Add more cheese, then more turnips, etc. Continue layering in this fashion, finishing with turnips. Mix together the crème fraîche, the remaining cheese and some seasoning and pour it over the vegetables. Bake for 30–35 minutes, until golden and bubbling. Turn out of the dish and leave to cool slightly before cutting into wedges.

PG TIPS Vary the layers of the torte with your favorite vegetables. It is very versatile and can be made in advance and cooked when needed.

Wild Mushroom and Potato Matafaim

9 oz. new potatoes

1/2 stick (1/4 cup) unsalted butter

1 banana shallot, chopped

1/4 lb. mixed wild mushrooms,
   cleaned (see page 172)

2 tablespoons chopped fresh parsley

1/2 cup all purpose flour

2 eggs, separated

2/3 cup milk

A pinch of sugar

Salt and freshly ground black pepper

Matafaim, meaning 'to beat hunger', is a potato dish eaten by farmers in the south of France after they have brought in the harvest. Traditionally it is torn with forks to serve.

Preheat the oven to 375°F. Boil the potatoes in their skins until just tender. Drain and allow to cool slightly, then peel and cut into slices 1/2-inch thick.

Heat half the butter in an 8-inch ovenproof frying pan and sauté the potato slices for about 4–5 minutes on each side, until golden. Remove from the pan and keep warm. Add the remaining butter to the pan, then add the shallot and wild mushrooms and sauté over a high heat until tender. Add half the parsley, season to taste, then set aside.

Sift the flour into a bowl, then beat in the egg yolks, milk and a pinch of salt to make a smooth batter. In a separate bowl, whisk the egg whites to a snow with the sugar, then fold them into the batter.

Return the potatoes to the mushroom pan and raise the heat. Pour the batter in, and tilt the pan to let it run under the vegetables and spread evenly. Transfer to the oven and cook for 8–10 minutes, until puffy and golden. Tear into pieces with the aid of 2 forks and transfer to a serving bowl. Garnish with the remaining parsley and serve.

fungi

Fungi such as wild mushrooms and truffles are some of the strangest yet most delicious foods available to us. These beautiful, aromatic plants feed off living or decaying organic matter by sending a huge web of tiny filaments (mycelium) underground through which they draw in nutrients. Their unpredictable growing habits mean that most of them are impossible to cultivate, hence their sometimes astronomical price and varying availability.

There are hundreds of edible species of fungi (and many more poisonous ones) but only a handful are highly sought after: the exquisite apricot-colored chanterelle; the dramatically dark trompette de mort –

Blewitt mushroom (left)

less scarily known as the horn of plenty; the sweet, nutty Boletus edulis, called cep in France and porcini in Italy; and, perhaps most precious of all, the morel – shaped like a date, with a distinctive honey-combed surface and a rich, powerful flavor.

Like all good things, wild mushrooms should be cooked simply. Their unique flavors are best appreciated in sautés, broths, with eggs, or as a sauce for chicken or fish. Cultivated mushrooms don't offer the same thrill as wild ones but they are much more interesting than they used to be. Once all we could buy was the bland button mushroom but now nut-brown chestnut mushrooms and meaty, black-gilled field mushrooms are just as easy to obtain and their flavor is ten times better. Two oriental mushrooms, the oyster and the shiitake, have recently been cultivated successfully, with a consequent drop in price and increase in availability.

Truffles have attained almost mythical status. There are very few gastronomic mysteries left but truffle propagation is one of them, since no one can predict where they will appear from one year to the next. Consequently both black and white varieties command a dizzyingly high price. Most people who are lucky enough to sample a fresh truffle, however, are totally smitten by its incomparable flavor and heady, lingering scent.

Blewitt mushrooms

Chestnut mushrooms

Portabello mushrooms

Wild mushrooms

Morels

Black truffles

White truffles

Wild Mushroom Potato Pan Pizza

2 medium floury baking potatoes,
    such as Russet
2 cups all purpose flour
2/3 cup milk
1 teaspoon dried yeast
1 1/2 teaspoons sugar
Salt and freshly ground black pepper

For the topping:
1/2 stick (1/4 cup) unsalted butter
1 shallot, finely chopped
1 garlic clove, crushed
3/4 lb. mixed wild mushrooms,
    such as trompettes, oyster
    mushrooms and girolles, cleaned
    (see page 172)
5 oz. buffalo mozzarella, grated
    (around 1 1/4 cups)

This pizza is made of a light potato dough topped with wild mushrooms and buffalo mozzarella.

Preheat the oven to 400°F. Wrap the potatoes in foil and bake for 1 hour or until tender. Remove from the foil and leave until cool enough to handle, then peel. Push through a strainer, then weigh the potato; you will need 7 oz. Leave to cool.

In a bowl, mix together the cold potato, flour and some salt and pepper. Heat the milk to lukewarm, then add the yeast and sugar and whisk until the yeast has dissolved. Set aside until it froths.

Stir the yeast mixture into the potato mixture and combine to form a dough. Turn out on to a floured work surface and knead for 5–8 minutes, until smooth and elastic. Place in a clean bowl, cover with a towel and leave in a warm place for 1 1/4 hours or until doubled in size.

Turn the dough out again and punch it down. Roll it out to fit a deep 8–10 inch frying pan with an ovenproof handle. Put it in the pan and set aside.

For the topping, heat the butter in a frying pan, add the shallot and garlic and cook for 2 minutes. Add the mushrooms and sauté for 4–5 minutes, then season to taste.

Distribute the mushroom mixture over the pizza dough, then sprinkle over it the grated mozzarella. Bake for 15–20 minutes, until crisp and golden. Serve straight from the oven, with a crisp salad.

Braised Pea Eggplants, Persian-style

2/3 cup olive oil

1 lb. small pea eggplants, cut lengthways in half (or large eggplants cut into large wedges)

1 onion, finely sliced

2 garlic cloves, crushed

4 teaspoons chopped fresh coriander leaves

1/2 teaspoon ground cumin

1/2 teaspoon ground allspice

4 plum tomatoes, skinned, seeded and chopped

1 1/2 teaspoons harissa paste

2 tablespoons pomegranate syrup

Juice of 1/2 lemon

1 1/4 cups water

1 pomegranate, halved, seeds removed

Salt

Of all the recipes in this book, this is undoubtedly my favorite. Pea eggplants are a tiny, roundish, purple or white variety, known in Thailand as makua phuong. Pomegranate syrup is available in some delicatessens and makes all the difference to this Middle Eastern-flavored dish.

Heat half the oil in a large frying pan, add the eggplant and fry for 3–4 minutes on each side, until lightly golden. Remove from the pan and set aside.

Heat the remaining oil in the pan, add the onion and garlic and fry over a moderate heat for 2 minutes, until softened and just beginning to brown. Add the coriander leaves, cumin, allspice, tomatoes and harissa and cook for 2 minutes. Stir in the pomegranate syrup, lemon juice and water and bring to a boil. Return the eggplant to the pan, lower the heat, then cover and simmer for 15–20 minutes or until the eggplant is tender and the sauce is thickish and syrupy in consistency. Season with salt, then scatter the pomegranate seeds over it. Serve with buttery couscous.

'pasta
provides the
perfect foil
for the
flavor of
portobello
mushrooms'

Penne with Roasted Portobello Mushrooms and Artichoke Sauce

3/4 lb. portobello mushrooms,
   cut into slices 1/4 in. thick
12 garlic cloves, peeled
2 tablespoons olive oil
1 lb. penne pasta
2 tablespoons unsalted butter
2 tablespoons freshly grated
   Parmesan cheese
Salt and freshly ground black pepper

For the sauce:
4 cooked artichoke bottoms
1 tablespoon freshly grated
   Parmesan cheese
6 tablespoons olive oil
1 garlic clove, chopped

The common brown or portobello mushrooms are a fairly new addition to our supermarket shelves. In North America and Italy they are greatly prized for their meaty flavor. The larger they are, the more intense the flavor becomes.

Preheat the oven to 375°F. Put the portobello mushrooms in a roasting pan with the garlic cloves, pour over them the olive oil and season with salt and pepper. Roast for 15–20 minutes, until the mushrooms are tender and the garlic is caramelized.
   Meanwhile, make the sauce: put the artichokes, cheese, 2 tablespoons of the oil and the garlic in a blender and blitz to a purée. Then blend in the rest of the oil and season with salt and pepper.
   Cook the penne in plenty of boiling salted water until al dente, then drain well. Return to the pot, add the butter and then add the artichoke sauce. Toss with the pasta. Season to taste, then transfer to a serving bowl and top with the roasted portobellos and garlic. Finally, sprinkle the Parmesan over them and serve.

PG TIPS For a real treat, you could substitute wild mushrooms for the portobellos.

Butternut Squash and Toasted Corn Gratin

2 corn on the cob, husks removed
1/2 cup virgin olive oil
1 lb. butternut squash, peeled,
   seeded and cut into 1/2 in.
   dice
1/2 tablespoon unsalted butter
1 teaspoon cumin seeds, toasted
2 small chiles, seeded and cut
   into rings
14-oz. can of unsweetened
   coconut milk
2 tablespoons fresh white
   breadcrumbs
Salt and freshly ground black pepper

A simple, spicy gratin that is surprisingly quick to make. The coconut milk adds an exotically creamy touch.

Preheat the oven to 400°F. Brush the corn with a little of the oil and then roast for about 30 minutes, until lightly browned. Leave to cool. Put the butternut squash on a baking sheet and toss with half the olive oil, then roast for 10–15 minutes, until just tender. Lightly grease a gratin dish with the butter and arrange the butternut squash in it. Season to taste.
   Scrape the corn kernels off the cobs with a sharp knife. Mix together the corn, cumin and chiles and sprinkle them over the squash. Pour the coconut milk over this, then scatter the breadcrumbs on top. Drizzle over the remaining oil and bake for 20–25 minutes, until the crust is browned and crisp.

Spaghetti with Creamed Purple Kale, Gorgonzola and Truffle

1 lb. purple curly kale
1/2 stick (1/4 cup) unsalted butter
2 garlic cloves, crushed
1/2 cup heavy cream
1 lb. spaghetti
3 oz. gorgonzola cheese,
    crumbled (around 3/4 cup)
2 tablespoons truffle oil
2 tablespoons olive oil
1 fresh black truffle, thinly sliced
Salt and freshly ground black pepper

Pasta is considered fast food nowadays, quick and easy to prepare and generally inexpensive. This recipe, however, is for a special occasion, when you can afford to splash out a little.

Remove the central stalks from the kale and shred the leaves into large pieces. Cook in a large pot of boiling salted water until just tender, then drain, reserving approximately 2/3 cup of the cooking water.

Melt the butter in another pot over a medium heat, add the garlic and cooked kale and raise the heat until all the liquid has evaporated. Add the reserved cooking water and the cream and simmer until reduced to half its volume.

Meanwhile, cook the pasta in plenty of boiling salted water until al dente. Drain well, add to the kale and toss together. Add the crumbled gorgonzola, the truffle oil and the olive oil. Season to taste.

Transfer to a serving bowl, scatter the thinly sliced truffle over it and serve immediately.

PG TIPS It is important to cook pasta just before you serve it. Fill a very large pot with water, add a little salt and bring to a boil. Cook the pasta until it is al dente, which literally means 'to the teeth' – i.e. it should retain a little bite. Dried pasta takes considerably longer to cook than fresh, about 8–10 minutes compared with 2–3 minutes. Always drain the pasta thoroughly before adding other ingredients.

Stuffed Cabbage Rolls
with Tahini Dressing

8 large white cabbage leaves

3 tablespoons olive oil

1 onion, chopped

2 garlic cloves, crushed

A pinch each of ground cumin, allspice and paprika

3/4 lb. ground lamb

1 tablespoon chopped fresh mint

1 cup cooked basmati rice

2 1/2 cups chicken stock

Salt and freshly ground black pepper

For the tahini dressing:

6 tablespoons olive oil

1 garlic clove, crushed

Juice of 2 lemons

1 tablespoon tahini

A pinch of ground cumin

1 tablespoon chopped fresh parsley

If you substitute chopped sautéed mushrooms for the meat and replace the chicken stock with vegetable stock, this makes a wonderful vegetarian dish.

Preheat the oven to 350°F. Plunge the cabbage leaves into a large pot of boiling salted water and simmer for about 4–5 minutes to make them pliable. Drain them well. Spread them out on a flat surface and cut out the central cores.

To make the stuffing, heat the oil in a large frying pan, add the onion, garlic and spices and cook until golden. Add the lamb, mint and some salt and pepper and cook for 10–12 minutes. Stir in the rice, then leave to cool slightly.

Place a portion of stuffing on each leaf, fold over the end, then fold in the sides and roll up into a neat roll. Arrange them close together in a greased shallow ovenproof dish and pour the stock over so that they are almost covered. Cover the dish, place in the oven and cook for 30 minutes or until the leaves are tender.

Meanwhile, prepare the dressing by whisking together all the ingredients. When the cabbage rolls are done, drain off the juices and mix them into the dressing. Pour the dressing over the cabbage and serve.

PG TIPS You can prepare the cabbage rolls a day in advance, then pour the stock over and cook them just before serving.

Asian Stir-fry Noodles
with Warm Tamarind Dressing

9 oz. oriental egg noodles

1 tablespoon sesame oil

1 tablespoon vegetable oil

2 carrots, cut into fine strips

2 heaped cups of broccoli flowerets

**1/4 lb. oyster mushrooms (around 1
    heaped cup)**

**1/4 lb. sugarsnap peas (around 1
    large handful**

1 1/2 cups beansprouts

**1/4 cucumber, peeled, halved length-
    ways, seeded and cut into fine
    strips**

For the dressing:

1 tablespoon tamarind paste

1 tablespoon sugar

Juice of 2 limes

2 red chiles, seeded and chopped

**1/2 in. piece of fresh ginger,
    grated**

**2 tablespoons ketjap manis
    (Indonesian soy sauce)**

1 tablespoon sesame oil

1 tablespoon chili oil

1/2 lemongrass stalk, finely chopped

Mix together all the ingredients for the dressing and set aside. Cook the egg noodles in boiling salted water for 2 minutes, then drain well through a colander.

Heat the sesame oil and vegetable oil in a wok or large frying pan over a high heat, add the carrots and broccoli and stir-fry for 1–2 minutes. Add the remaining vegetables and stir-fry for 1–2 minutes longer. Add the egg noodles and toss together.

Pour in the tamarind dressing and toss well to coat the vegetables and noodles. Heat through for 1 minute, then serve.

Spring Vegetable Bourride
with Herb Aïoli

3 tablespoons olive oil

**2 lb. mixed spring vegetables
(such as baby leeks, broccoli, baby
zucchini, sugarsnap peas, baby
carrots, asparagus and morel
mushrooms), trimmed and cut into
bite-sized pieces if necessary**

1 quart chicken stock

For the herb aïoli:

2 egg yolks

4 garlic cloves, crushed

Juice of 1/2 lemon

1/2 cup virgin olive oil

1/2 cup peanut oil

**1/2 tablespoon finely chopped fresh
chives**

**1/2 tablespoon finely chopped fresh
basil**

**1 teaspoon finely chopped fresh
tarragon**

Salt and freshly ground black pepper

Bourride is a mixed fish stew thickened with garlic mayonnaise (aïoli). Here I have prepared a vegetable bourride based on the same technique.

First make the aïoli. Mix the egg yolks, garlic, lemon juice and seasoning together in a bowl. Put the olive oil and peanut oil in a jar and add them to the bowl in a very slow trickle, whisking constantly. When all the oil has been added you should have a thick, glossy emulsion that clings to the whisk. Stir in the herbs and set to one side.

Heat the oil in a large pot, add the leeks and broccoli and sauté for 2 minutes. Add the remaining vegetables and toss together. Pour in the stock, bring to a boil, then reduce the heat and cook for 8–10 minutes or until the vegetables are tender. Transfer the vegetables to a dish with a slotted spoon and keep warm.

Strain the cooking liquid and then return it to the pot over a very gentle heat. Add the aïoli and whisk until almost at boiling point (do not let it boil or the sauce will curdle). Season to taste, then return the vegetables to the sauce and transfer to a serving dish. Serve immediately.

PG TIPS For the best results, make sure all the ingredients for the aïoli are at room temperature. You could use a food processor instead of doing it by hand but the oil should be added with care in the same manner.

vegetable
fruits

Vegetable fruits such as eggplants, peppers and tomatoes epitomize the Mediterranean diet, whether it's the 101 eggplant dishes of Turkey, the indispensable tomato sauces of Italy or the colorful pepper stews of Spain. Yet surprisingly they are all relative newcomers to the area. Eggplants have a much longer history in Africa and Asia, from where they were brought to Europe in the Middle Ages. The eggplant of the Mediterranean is the familiar plump, oval, deep-purple variety but in the Far East you are just as likely to see small, round ones that are green, yellow or white in color. Both peppers and tomatoes were brought back to Europe from America in the sixteenth century and at first were

White aubergines (left)

regarded with deep suspicion everywhere. Tomatoes especially were considered dangerous, yet from the late eighteenth century they began to be accepted and in Italy in particular they quickly became an essential part of the cuisine. Now many areas of southern Europe feature these vegetable fruits in their national dish: ratatouille in Provence, caponata in Sicily and escalivada in Spain.

It's fortunate that the inhabitants of the Mediterranean did finally take to eggplants, peppers and tomatoes, for they have a wonderful affinity with olive oil, not to mention other essential flavorings such as garlic, anchovies and capers. Nowadays many of the vegetable fruits we eat are grown in Northern Europe and so have been deprived of the daily dose of sunshine that gives them their incomparable flavor. One consolation is the recent popularity of roasting and chargrilling – techniques that maximize their sweetness and give the flesh a melting succulence. Cucumbers have a slightly different culinary role. Countries from the UK and Denmark to India, Egypt, Greece and Spain capitalize on their refreshing qualities, serving them in salads, chilled soups or simple sautés.

Avocados

Chayote

Chilies

Chinese melon

Cucumbers

White eggplant

Peppers

Tomatoes

Eggplant

Fricassee of Wild Mushrooms
with Walnuts, Prunes and Thyme

9 oz. porcini mushrooms
9 oz. chanterelle or girolle
mushrooms
1/4 cup virgin olive oil
2 garlic cloves, crushed
5 tablespoons Madeira wine
2 1/2 cups well-flavored chicken
stock
2 sprigs of fresh thyme
12 Agen prunes, pitted
10-12 walnut halves
1 teaspoon truffle oil (optional)
1/2 stick (1/4 cup) unsalted butter,
chilled anddiced
Salt and freshly ground black pepper

This makes a superb vegetarian treat if you substitute vegetable stock for the chicken stock. Fresh wild mushrooms have an exquisite flavor but if necessary you could replace some of them with reconstituted dried mushrooms. Occasionally I like to top toasted brioche with this mixture.

Clean the mushrooms by wiping them with a damp cloth. Separate the porcini stems from the caps, removing the soft underpart of the cap if it is too spongy. Peel the stems and cut into slices 1/4-inch thick. Cut the caps into large pieces, depending on their size.

Heat half the olive oil in a frying pan, add the garlic and cook for 4–5 minutes, until lightly golden. Add the porcini stems and sauté for a minute or two. Add the Madeira and chicken stock and cook for 5 minutes. Transfer to a blender and blitz until smooth. Pour into a saucepan and keep warm.

Wipe out the frying pan and heat the remaining olive oil in it over a high heat. Add the porcini caps and chanterelles and sauté for 5 minutes, then add the leaves from the thyme sprigs (reserving some for garnish) and the prunes and cook for 2–3 minutes. Stir in the walnuts.

Reheat the sauce but do not let it boil. Add the truffle oil, if using, and then whisk in the butter a few pieces at a time. Season to taste. Pile the mushrooms and prunes on to individual serving plates and surround with the sauce. Garnish with a little fresh thyme and serve immediately.

Marinated and Broiled
Teriyaki Shiitakes

²/₃ cup sake
¹/₄ cup teriyaki sauce
2 tablespoons mirin
2 tablespoons dark brown sugar
¹/₂ garlic clove, crushed
1 tablespoon sesame oil
24 large shiitake mushrooms

This recipe uses mirin, a Japanese sweet rice wine that is usually added to sauces or marinades for meats and strong-tasting fish such as tuna. Shiitake mushrooms, with their distinctive meaty flavor, make a wonderful vegetarian alternative, easy to prepare and great served with oriental noodles.

You will need 4 bamboo skewers for this recipe, soaked in cold water for 30 minutes–1 hour before use to prevent them burning.

Put all the ingredients except the mushrooms in a pan and bring to a boil. Reduce to a simmer, add the mushrooms and cook for 1 minute. Transfer everything to a bowl and leave to marinate for up to 1 hour.

Thread the shiitakes on to bamboo skewers, allowing 6 mushrooms per skewer. Cook under a hot broiler for 3–4 minute or until lightly charred, turning as necessary and brushing the mushrooms occasionally with the marinade. Serve immediately.

PG TIPS Sesame oil should not be heated to too high a temperature as it has a tendency to become bitter.

Salsifis Forestière (Salsify and Wild Mushrooms with Truffle Oil)

12 salsify
1 quart water
3 tablespoons white wine vinegar
¹/₂ stick (¹/₄ cup) unsalted butter
1 tablespoon lemon juice
2 cups well-flavored
   chicken stock
5 oz. girolle mushrooms,
   cleaned (see page 172)
3 oz. trompette mushrooms,
   cleaned (see page 172)
1 tablespoon white truffle oil
Salt and freshly ground black pepper

Salsify are delicious served cold with lemon and olive oil dressing or eaten like asparagus. They also make a lovely creamy soup. One of my favorite ways of eating them is topped with cheese sauce, preferably after being wrapped in thin slices of ham.

Wash the salsify well and scrub with a small nailbrush to remove the dirt. Put the water and vinegar in a bowl, then peel the salsify and place them in the water – this will help prevent them discoloring. Cut the salsify into 2-inch lengths and dry them.

Heat the butter in a sauté pan, add the salsify and lemon juice and sweat for 1 minute. Add the stock and season with salt and pepper. Bring to a boil, then reduce the heat and simmer for 10 minutes.

Add the wild mushrooms, mix with the salsify and raise the heat to a full boil, until the vegetables are lightly glazed by the sauce. Finally add the truffle oil, taste and correct the seasoning, then serve.

'a rich
profusion
of Middle-
Eastern
spiced
vegetables'

Fire-roasted Vegetables with Tabil

2 fennel bulbs, each cut into 6 pieces
   lengthways
1 red pepper, cut into 6 strips
1 yellow pepper, cut into 6 strips
3 small red onions, cut into quarters
1 eggplant, cut into 2 in. chunks
3 medium zucchini, cut into slices
   1/2 in. thick
4 tomatoes
1/2 cup olive oil
Salt and freshly ground black pepper

For the tabil:
1 tablespoon coriander seeds
1 teaspoon caraway seeds
2 garlic cloves, crushed
1/8 teaspoon cayenne pepper
1/8 teaspoon curry powder
1/2 teaspoon ground cumin
2/3 cup olive oil

Tabil is a heady Middle Eastern spice mix used with fish, meat and vegetables. You could choose any selection of vegetables for this fragrant dish. Serve with couscous.

Preheat the oven to 400°F. Place all the vegetables in a bowl and toss with the oil, then grill on a barbecue or ridged grill pan for 10 minutes, turning occasionally, until charred.

Meanwhile, mix all the ingredients for the tabil together in a large bowl. Add the vegetables to the tabil and leave to marinate for 30 minutes, then put all the vegetables, except the tomatoes, in a baking dish with the marinade. Season to taste. Transfer to the oven and bake for 30–35 minutes, basting frequently with the juices. Add the tomatoes just before the completion of cooking. Serve hot from the oven.

on the side

This is the longest chapter in the book, which reflects my unbounded enthusiasm for vegetable accompaniments! Some of these recipes are extremely simple to prepare but they really add color and excitement to a meal – whether by using an unexpected flavor combination, such as Gingerbread-spiced Parsnips (page 134), or by dressing up an unglamorous vegetable with rich ingredients – Button Sprouts with Parmesan and Pearl Onions on page 144, for example. Much as I enjoy experimenting, I'm also very fond of old favorites, such as gratins, mashes and simple braised and roast vegetable dishes, so there are plenty of those here. Plus a few simple preserves and relishes, which are particularly useful if you have a glut of vegetables to deal with.

Broccoli with Anchovies and Parsley, the Sicilian Way

5 tablespoons olive oil

1 lb., 5oz. broccoli, divided into flowerets

1 onion, thinly sliced

12 canned anchovy fillets, rinsed, drained and finely chopped

2 tablespoons chopped fresh flat-leaf parsley

1/2 cup water

2/3 cup dry white wine

Salt and freshly ground black pepper

The Italians love broccoli and have so many different ways of cooking it. One of the best is with anchovies, whose saltiness adds zest to its somewhat bland flavour. The broccoli in this recipe should be thoroughly cooked; don't be tempted to leave it al dente.

Heat the olive oil in a large sauté pan and add the broccoli flowerets. Scatter over them the onion, anchovies and parsley, then season with salt and a good amount of pepper. Add the water, cover with a tight-fitting lid and cook over a low heat for 10 minutes.

Add the wine, increase the heat and remove the lid. Leave to cook for 5 minutes, until nearly all the liquid has evaporated.

PG TIPS Never throw away broccoli stalks. They are excellent made into soups, added to stir-fries or deep-fried in a crisp batter coating.

Fava Beans and Salsify with Garlic Cream

9 oz. shelled fresh baby fava beans (or fresh shelled peas)

2 tablespoons unsalted butter

2 garlic cloves, crushed

2 shallots, finely chopped

3/4 lb. salsify, peeled and cut into 1 in. lengths

2/3 cup vegetable stock

2/3 cup heavy cream

1 tablespoon chopped fresh mint

1 tablespoon lemon juice

Salt and freshly ground black pepper

The only slight disadvantage to preparing this dish is the patience needed to peel these delicate beans, but the end result is well worth the effort. (When not in season, most chefs, myself included, are happy to use frozen fava beans . The quality is good as they are picked, shelled and frozen over a very short period to ensure none of the flavor is lost.)

Bring a large pot of water to a boil, add the fava beans and simmer for 5 minutes. Drain them and peel off the skins, then set aside.

Heat the butter in a pan, add the garlic and shallots and sweat for 5 minutes. Add the salsify, pour in the stock and cream and bring to a boil. Reduce the heat and simmer for 12–15 minutes or until the salsify are tender. Remove the salsify with a slotted spoon and boil the cooking liquid until reduced and slightly thickened. Stir in the mint and lemon juice and season to taste. Return the salsify to the sauce with the fava beans, reheat gently and serve.

'vegetables in garlic cream - a marriage made in heaven'

Charred Green Beans
with Red Onion Sambal

11 oz. young green beans
1 garlic clove, crushed
4 teaspoons peanut oil
Salt and freshly ground black pepper

For the sambal:
2 red onions, thinly sliced
3 tablespoons rice wine vinegar
1/4 cup apricot jam
1 red chile, seeded and finely
   chopped
2 tablespoons chopped fresh
   coriander leaves
1 tablespoon chopped fresh mint

For those of you who love plainly cooked vegetables, chargrilling French beans may seem a little strange. I find, however, that they take on a unique smoky flavor which, when mixed with the sambal, brings forth a perfect marriage of tastes and textures.

For the sambal, place the onions in a bowl, season with salt and leave for 20 minutes to draw out the moisture. Rinse well and dry.

In another bowl combine the vinegar, jam and chile. Add the onions and herbs and mix well. Leave to marinate for 1 hour.

Cook the green beans in boiling salted water for about 3–4 minutes, until just tender, then drain them. Mix the garlic and oil together with a little salt and pepper, toss the beans in the mixture, then put them on a ridged grill pan or under a preheated broiler and cook for 2 minutes or until lightly charred. Place in a serving bowl and toss with the red onion sambal to serve.

Oven-fried Celeriac Chips
with Tartar Sauce

2 large celeriac, peeled
1/2 cup vegetable oil
Celery salt

For the tartar sauce:
1/2 cup mayonnaise
1 teaspoon Dijon mustard
1 tablespoon finely chopped gherkins
1 tablespoon superfine capers
1 tablespoon chopped fresh
   coriander leaves
Salt and freshly ground black pepper

This does away with the hassle of deep-frying. Celeriac has a wonderful nutty flavor and makes a nice change from potato fries.

Preheat the oven to 400°F. Cut the celeriac into thick, old-fashioned chips. Put a heavy roasting pan in the oven for 10 minutes, then carefully pour in the vegetable oil (it will spit). Return it to the oven and heat for 2 minutes. Carefully add the celeriac to the hot oil and cook for 30 minutes, turning regularly, until golden on all sides.

Meanwhile, mix together all the ingredients for the tartar sauce, seasoning to taste.

When the chips are crisp and golden, drain on paper towels, season with celery salt and serve with the tartar sauce as a dip.

Baby New Potatoes in Rock Salt Crust

1/2 lb. rock salt

3 egg whites

2 oz. fresh rosemary sprigs (around 8 9-inch sprigs)

8 garlic cloves, peeled

I lb. small new potatoes, well scrubbed

Baking tiny new potatoes in a salt crust may seem a little excessive. However, not only does it make for an unusual and dramatic presentation but the sealed-in flavors become really intensified – moist and garlicky without being excessively salty.

Preheat the oven to 450°F. In a bowl mix the salt, egg whites, rosemary sprigs and garlic together. Take a baking dish large enough to hold the potatoes in a single layer and spread a thin layer of the salt mixture over the base. Top with the potatoes and cover completely with the remaining salt mixture.

Bake for 30–35 minutes, until the crust is golden brown and risen. Leave to cool slightly and then crack the crust open with a kitchen hammer or a heavy knife to release the steamy hot potatoes. Brush off the salt and serve.

Yellow Wax Beans with Chinese Parsley Oil

2 oz. fresh coriander leaves (a good quarter-bunch)

2 tablespoons unsalted butter

2 tablespoons olive oil

1 lb. yellow wax beans

Salt and freshly ground black pepper

Yellow wax beans are a very underused vegetable. Not only do they taste great when simply seasoned with salt, lots of pepper and butter but they are also very versatile. Try mixing them with young green beans and legumes, either hot or in a salad. Here they are tossed with a light Chinese parsley oil. Chinese parsley is another term for coriander leaves (also known as cilantro), which is used in Asian cookery as a staple herb in the way that we would use parsley.

Blanch the coriander leaves in a large pot of boiling water for 30 seconds, then drain and refresh under cold running water. Dry in a lintfree towel.

Heat the butter and oil in a frying pan and stir in the coriander leaves. Transfer to a blender and blitz to a purée. Return the mixture to the frying pan.

Cook the beans in a large pot of boiling water until tender but still crisp, about 3–5 minutes. Drain them well and add to the frying pan. Toss with the coriander mixture, season with salt and pepper and serve immediately.

'this typical feast of flavors from North Africa is one of my favorite vegetable dishes'

Carrots and Beets
with North African Spices

12 very small beets
1/4 cup olive oil
6 carrots, cut into slices 1/2 in.
   thick
1/2 stick (1/4 cup) unsalted butter
1/4 teaspoon ground coriander
1/4 teaspoon cumin seeds
1/4 teaspoon ground cinnamon
1 teaspoon lemon zest
1 teaspoon light brown sugar
A pinch of saffron strands, soaked in
   2 tablespoons hot water for 10
   minutes
1 teaspoon finely chopped coriander
   root (well washed), if available
1 tablespoon chopped fresh mint
Salt and freshly ground black pepper

A typical feast of flavors from North Africa. Coriander roots are often cut off and thrown away – what a pity, as they are very fragrant and make a valuable addition to sauces and soups.

Preheat the oven to 375°F. Wash and trim the beets, leaving 1-inch of the top attached, but do not peel them. Place in a shallow baking dish, pour the oil over, then cover with foil and bake until tender when pierced with a small knife, about 40–50 minutes. Uncover and leave to cool for 15 minutes, then peel them and cut in half vertically.

   Cook the carrots in boiling salted water until just tender, then drain and refresh under cold running water.

   Melt the butter in a large frying pan, add the spices, lemon zest, sugar and saffron and cook for 1 minute. Add the beets and carrots and the coriander root, if using, and toss together gently. Season to taste, transfer to a serving dish and sprinkle the mint over them before serving.

PG TIPS Paring the zest of lemons or other citrus fruits is simple if you use a small tool called, believe it or not, a zester. This removes fine strands of peel but leaves the pith intact so it doesn't taste bitter. You could also use a potato peeler but you may have to cut away a little pith from the zest and then cut the zest into shreds.

Red Onion Wedges with Honey Ginger Glaze

8-12 small red onions
2/3 cup liquid honey
1 in. piece of fresh ginger,
   grated
1/2 cup white wine vinegar
2/3 cup water
Salt and freshly ground black pepper

These sweet glazed onion wedges make an ideal accompaniment to spicy barbecued meat dishes.

Peel the onions and cut each one into 6 wedges, keeping the root intact.

   Heat the honey in a pan, add the onion wedges and ginger, and cook over a low heat until lightly caramelized. Pour in the vinegar and stir gently to release the caramel, then dilute with the water. Simmer over a low heat until the onions are very tender and the liquid has totally evaporated. Season to taste and and serve.

Hush Puppies

Makes about 20

**a generous cup fine yellow cornmeal
or polenta**
**1/2 cup, plus 2 tablespoons all pur-
pose flour**
2 tablespoons sugar
1 1/2 teaspoons baking powder
1/2 teaspoon cayenne pepper
**1/2 cup buttermilk or whole
milk**
1 egg
**1/2 cup corn (frozen or canned will
do)**
4 scallions, finely shredded
Vegetable oil for deep-frying
Salt and freshly ground black pepper

Hush puppies are delicate, spicy fritters of onion and corn that origi-
nate from the Southern US states. The story goes that, to keep
hungry dogs from begging for food while dinner was being prepared,
cooks used to toss scraps of fried batter to them with the admoni-
tion, 'Hush, puppies!'

Place the cornmeal, flour, sugar, baking powder and cayenne in a
bowl. Add the buttermilk or milk, egg, corn, scallions and seasoning
and mix together well. Cover with plastic wrap and refrigerate
overnight.
   Pour enough vegetable oil into a large pot to reach a depth of 3
inches – or use a deep-fat fryer – and heat to 350°F.
Drop tablespoonfuls of the batter into the hot oil, being careful not to
overcrowd the pot, and cook for about 3–4 minutes, turning them
once, until golden brown. Drain on paper towels and keep warm
while you make the rest. Serve immediately.

Cajun Hash Browns

1 1/2 lbs. potatoes, cut into 1/2 in. dice
1/2 teaspoon sweet paprika
1/2 teaspoon chili powder
**1 teaspoon Cajun seasoning (see Tip
on page 22)**
1 small onion, grated
1/4 cup olive oil
**4-5 strips bacon, finely
chopped**
4 scallions, shredded
1 cup grated Cheddar cheese
1/4 cup sour cream
Salt

An American breakfast favorite of crisp fried potatoes, here given a
Southern twist with Cajun spices. Hash browns are not just breakfast
fare. Serve them for lunch with a crisp green salad.

Preheat the oven to 375°F. Cook the potatoes in boiling salted water
until almost tender, then drain well and place in a bowl. Sprinkle over
them the spices, cajun seasoning, grated onion and some salt, then
crush lightly.
   Heat the oil in an ovenproof frying pan, add the bacon and fry until
crisp. Add the potato mixture and stir lightly together. Transfer the
pan to the oven and cook until crisp, turning occasionally, about
15–20 minutes.
   Top the mixture with the shredded scallions, sprinkle over them
the cheese and return it to the oven to glaze until golden and bubbling. Transfer to a cutting board, cool slightly, then cut into 4
wedges and serve with the sour cream.

Masala Green Beans with Yoghurt Sauce

1 lb. young green beans
1 tablespoon sesame oil
1 tablespoon vegetable oil
1/2 teaspoon cumin seeds
1/2 teaspoon mustard seeds
1/2 teaspoon cardamom seeds
1/4 teaspoon ground turmeric
5 tablespoons Greek yoghurt, or
    thick whole milk yoghurt
1/2 garlic clove, crushed
1/2 teaspoon garam masala
Salt and freshly ground black pepper

Cook the green beans in boiling salted water until just tender but still slightly crisp, then drain well.

Heat both the oils in a frying pan, add the cumin, mustard seeds, cardamom and turmeric and stir for a few seconds. Add the yoghurt and garlic and simmer for 1–2 minutes, then add the green beans and garam masala. Toss together, adjust the seasoning and cook until the beans are coated in the yoghurt sauce. Transfer to a serving dish and serve immediately.

PG TIPS Garam masala is a delicate spice mix, commonly made up of ground cumin, cinnamon, cloves, coriander and black pepper. It is easily available ready-made but its flavor is quickly lost when it sits on the shelf so it is best freshly ground. Always add garam masala towards the end of cooking so that the heat will not destroy its flavor.

Cider-glazed Baby Turnips with Golden Raisins

1/2 cup Californian golden raisins
1 cup dry (alcoholic) cider or 1/2 cup
    apple cider and 1/2 cup dry white
    wine
1 lb. baby turnips, scraped
    clean but tops left on
2 tablespoons sugar
2 tablespoons unsalted butter, cut
    into small pieces
1 apple (preferably Golden Delicious),
    peeled, cored and cut into small
    wedges
2 tablespoons cider vinegar
Salt and freshly ground black pepper

Place the raisins in a small bowl and cover with 5 tablespoons of the cider. Leave to macerate at room temperature while you cook the turnips.

Place the turnips in a shallow pan in which they fit in a single layer. Pour in the remaining cider and top up with cold water just to cover the turnips. Add the sugar, butter and some salt. Bring to a boil, then reduce the heat and cook gently until the turnips are tender. Remove the turnips from the pan with a slotted spoon, increase the heat to high and cook until the liquid is reduced and syrupy enough to form a glaze. Add the apple wedges and cider vinegar and cook until the apple is caramelized and tender, about 2–3 minutes. Return the turnips to the pan and turn the turnips and apple in the glaze.

Finally add the macerated raisins and cider to the turnips and toss together. Adjust the seasoning and serve.

Balsamic-glazed Red Chicory

1/4 cup olive oil

4 large, plump red chicory, trimmed
   and cut in half lengthways

1/2 cup balsamic vinegar

1 tablespoon redcurrant jelly

2 cups meat stock

Salt and freshly ground black pepper

The sweet balsamic glaze makes the perfect foil for the buttery chicory. The bitter-sweet flavors of this dish make it an excellent accompaniment to chicken, lamb or, my particular favorite, topped with crisply fried slices of calf's liver.

Heat the oil in a heavy-based pan over a low heat. Add the chicory and cook for 5–8 minutes, until it begins to wilt. Add the vinegar and redcurrant jelly, cover and cook for 8–10 minutes. Add the stock and some salt and pepper, raise the heat and continue cooking for 15 minutes.

Remove the chicory from the pan, fold each one in half by carefully turning over one end, then place in a serving dish. Strain any remaining syrupy juices from the pan and pour them over the chicory. Serve immediately.

PG TIPS This red chicory is not radicchio but rather a red-colored Belgian endive.

Gujerati-style Spinach
with Lemon and Black Pepper

2 tablespoons vegetable oil

1 garlic clove, crushed

1 teaspoon cumin seeds

2 1/4 lb. fresh spinach, well
   washed

Juice and zest of 1 lemon

1/2 teaspoon sugar

1/4 cup plain yoghurt

1/4 teaspoon black peppercorns,
   coarsely crushed

Salt

Heat the vegetable oil in a deep-sided frying pan, add the garlic and cumin seeds and fry for 1 minute to release their fragrance. Add the spinach, raise the heat and turn the spinach in the oil with the garlic and cumin. Add the lemon juice and zest and cook until the spinach has wilted. Stir in the sugar, yoghurt and black pepper and adjust the seasoning. Serve hot.

'lemon, cumin
and black
pepper –
the ideal
seasoning
for pan-wilted
spinach'

Sweet Potatoes Methi

3 tablespoons ghee or vegetable oil

1/2 teaspoon cumin seeds

1/2 teaspoon ground turmeric

1/2 teaspoon chili powder

1 1/4 lbs. white-fleshed sweet potatoes, cut into bite-sized chunks

1/2 teaspoon fenugreek seeds

2/3 cup water

1/2 teaspoon garam masala

2 tablespoons chopped fresh coriander leaves (optional)

Salt

These highly spiced sweet potatoes are an explosion of Far Eastern flavors. Methi is the Indian name for fenugreek, a pungent spice that is included in most curry powders. Serve as an accompaniment to an Indian-inspired meal.

Heat the ghee or oil in a pan, add the cumin seeds and fry until they pop. Stir in the turmeric and chili powder and cook for 30 seconds. Add the sweet potatoes, fenugreek seeds and water, cover with a lid and reduce the heat. Cook the potatoes slowly until they are tender, adding a little more water if necessary.

Sprinkle in the garam masala, salt and coriander leaves, if using, just before the end of the cooking time. Serve immediately.

PG TIPS Traditionally ghee would be used in this Indian dish. Ghee is basically clarified butter and adds great flavor to Indian food. It can be bought ready made or, to make your own, simmer some unsalted butter very gently for 20 minutes or until the solids at the bottom of the pan brown slightly. Strain through a piece of cheesecloth and leave to cool.

Spicy Corn in Coconut, Turmeric and Tomato Sauce

3 corn on the cob, husks removed

7 oz. block of unsweetened coconut cream (or canned, if unavailable)

4 plum tomatoes, skinned, seeded and chopped

1/4 teaspoon ground turmeric

1 garlic clove, crushed

1 green chile, seeded and finely chopped

1 tablespoon chopped fresh coriander leaves

Lemon juice, to taste

Salt and freshly ground black pepper

Cook the corn cobs in just enough water to cover until tender (around 5 minutes), then remove from the pan and cut into 2 inch lengths. Add the coconut cream to the cooking water and bring to a boil, stirring to dissolve. Add the tomatoes, turmeric, garlic and chile and simmer for 10 minutes before returning the corn to the sauce. Simmer for 15–20 minutes, then stir in the coriander leaves, lemon juice and seasoning and serve.

PG TIPS In some recipes turmeric can be substituted for saffron to give a golden color (unlike saffron, turmeric is one of the cheapest spices). A word of caution, though: do not use too much – it is musty and will easily overpower the dish.

Runner Beans
with Walnut and Bacon Gremolata

**1 lb. runner beans or Italian green
beans, sliced lengthways into
strips about 1/4 in. thick**
2 tablespoons unsalted butter
Salt and freshly ground black pepper

For the gremolata:
**1/4 lb. pancetta or bacon
cut into small strips**
3 cups fresh white breadcrumbs
1/2 stick (1/4 cup) unsalted butter
**1 tablespoon chopped fresh flat-leaf
parsley**
Zest of 1/2 lemon
1/2 cup coarsely ground walnuts

Runner beans are a lovely vegetable, much more versatile than you
might think. They have far too short a season, so use them while
stocks last! I sometimes like to add a little finely chopped hard-boiled
egg to the gremolata in this recipe, which works rather well.

Cook the beans in plenty of boiling salted water for 4–5 minutes,
then drain. Heat the butter in a shallow pan, add the beans and toss
together. Season with salt and pepper, then place in a serving dish
and keep warm while you prepare the gremolata.

Heat a heavy-based frying pan until slightly smoking, add the
bacon strips and fry until they are golden and have released their fat.
Add the breadcrumbs and butter and sauté until lightly golden and
crisp. Mix in the parsley and lemon zest, then add the walnuts and
season with salt and pepper. Spoon the gremolata over the beans
and serve immediately.

Cumin-scented Tomatoes

2 tablespoons vegetable oil
1 small onion, finely chopped
1/4 teaspoon ground turmeric
**1/4 teaspoon cumin seeds, lightly
crushed**
1/4 cup dry white wine
**1 lb. plum tomatoes, coarsely
chopped**
1 teaspoon light brown sugar
**2 tablespoons chopped fresh
coriander leaves**
Salt and freshly ground black pepper

A simple and versatile fondue of tomatoes with a touch of Indian
spicing. I normally serve this with grilled pork, or tossed with zucchini
as an accompaniment.

Heat the oil in a pan, add the onion and sauté over a low heat for 3–4
minutes, until softened. Add the turmeric and cumin seeds and cook
for 2 minutes. Stir in the wine and simmer over a moderate heat for 5
minutes, then add the tomatoes and sugar. Cook gently for about 10
minutes, until the tomatoes are soft but not mushy and the liquid has
reduced. Stir in the coriander leaves and season to taste.

**PG TIPS This dish is best prepared during the summer
months when tomatoes are sweet, juicy and succulent.
Canned tomatoes could be used instead but the flavor will
not be quite the same.**

pods & seeds

The vegetables in this group are the essence of summer eating – tiny, tender peas and fava beans, slim green beans and ripe, golden corn. With their lovely flowers and dainty, climbing tendrils, peas and beans make an attractive addition to any garden. Only people who grow their own (or know someone who does) can enjoy the true taste of these fragile summer vegetables. So however small your garden or patio, try to make space for them. Although frozen and canned peas and corn are available pretty much everywhere, and green beans and snow peas are air-freighted over from hot countries at vast expense throughout the year, the truth is they are at their best

Corn on the cob (left)

harvested when young and eaten within an hour or two of picking.

Shelling home-grown peas for Sunday lunch used to be a regular activity in many English households during the summer, a task usually delegated to children, who would end up eating as many peas as they put in the pan. Podding fava beans was a less popular chore, or stringing coarse runner beans, often grown until they were too leathery to enjoy. Now people are just as likely to have snow peas or sugarsnaps with their Sunday roast. Beloved of nouvelle cuisine chefs and busy home cooks alike, the whole pods look much prettier on the plate and are quicker to prepare. However, they rarely have the depth of flavor of young fresh peas.

Corn is the all-American vegetable, as indispensable to the American culinary tradition as peas are to the English and green beans to the French. The simplest way to serve it is on the cob, with plenty of butter, but it can also be roast, puréed or made into chowders, relishes and fritters.

Okra, too, has become part of America's culinary heritage, although it has a darker past. Brought to the States as part of the brutish slave trade from Africa, it is still used in the famous Cajun gumbo. Its sticky juice gives a distinctive silky texture to stews and curries throughout India and the Caribbean, too.

Fava beans

Green beans

Runner beans

Yellow wax beans

Corn

Corn on the cob

Okra

Peas

Snow peas

Sugarsnap peas

My Mother's Five-minute Onion Pudding

2 large onions, very thinly sliced
2¹/₄ cups self-rising flour
¹/₃ cup chopped suet
¹/₂ stick (¹/₄ cup) unsalted butter
Salt and freshly ground black pepper

When I was a teenager living at home, Sunday lunch was one of the highlights of my week. Although the food was plain, it was always delicious. This is my late mother's simple recipe for an onion pudding to serve with the Sunday roast, a recipe that she enjoyed as a child. Using a microwave cuts out the time-consuming steaming process.

Place the onions in a large bowl, add the flour and suet and season with salt and pepper. Add enough water to bind the ingredients into a soft but not sloppy mixture. Well butter 4 large ramekin dishes and fill with the mixture, tapping the dishes to ensure they are completely full.

Cover with plastic wrap and microwave on full power for 3 minutes or until cooked through; test by inserting a small knife into the center of the puddings – it should come out clean.

Leave to cool slightly, then turn the puddings out of the dishes. Heat the butter in a frying pan and sauté the puddings for about 2–3 minutes on each side, until golden and crisp. Serve immediately.

PG TIPS These puddings can be made a day in advance and fried just before needed. They also freeze well, I am told, but I wouldn't know as they are never around long enough to go in the freezer!

Sautéed Crosnes with Tarragon and Tangerines

1 lb. crosnes (Japanese
    artichokes), trimmed
¹/₂ stick (¹/₄ cup) unsalted butter
¹/₂ teaspoon sugar
Juice of 4 tangerines
Zest of 1 tangerine
1 tablespoon finely chopped fresh
    tarragon
Salt and freshly ground black pepper

Enthusiasts can grow their own crosnes, or Japanese artichokes (see picture opposite). Otherwise they can be purchased from good vegetable markets. If you cannot find any, replace with Jerusalem artichokes.

Blanch the artichokes in boiling water for 1 minute, then remove with a slotted spoon and place them on a lint free towel with a little salt. Rub them gently with the towel to remove the delicate skins. Rinse under cold water and pat dry.

Heat the butter in a small frying pan until foaming, then add the artichokes and sauté until just golden. Add the sugar and cook until the artichokes are lightly caramelized. Add the tangerine juice and zest and simmer until reduced to a thick syrup. Season with salt and pepper, then add the tarragon and toss all together. Serve immediately.

Rumbledethumps

2 large floury baking potatoes, such
as Russet, cut into small chunks
(about 1 lb. 10 oz. total weight)
1/2 lb. parsnips, cut into small
chunks (to yield around 2 cups)
3 tablespoons vegetable oil
1/2 stick (1/4 cup) unsalted butter
1 onion, finely chopped
1 heaped cup Brussels sprouts, base
removed, broken into individual
leaves (or use chopped cabbage)
1 egg, beaten
Flour for dusting
Salt and freshly ground black pepper

For the mustard butter:
1 tablespoon grainy mustard
1/2 stick (1/4 cup) unsalted butter
1 tablespoon chopped fresh parsley

Rumbledethumps is the strange name given to a type of Scottish 'bubble and squeak', a dish enjoying renewed popularity in the UK. I like to enliven it with some parsnip and top it with a mustard butter. 'Bubble and Squeak' consists of pan fried mashed potatoes with a cooked green vegetable, usually cabbage.

Place the potatoes and parsnips in a pot, cover with cold water and bring to a boil. Cook until tender, then drain well. Mash thoroughly, place in a bowl and leave to cool.

For the mustard butter, put all the ingredients in a bowl and beat together. Season, then place on a piece of wax paper, shape into a log and roll up in the paper. Place in the refrigerator for at least an hour to set hard.

Heat half the oil and butter in a frying pan, add the onion and fry until tender but not colored. Stir in the Brussels leaves and cook for 3–4 minutes, until wilted. Add this mixture to the potatoes and parsnips, season with salt and pepper and bind with the egg.

Shape the mixture into 4 large or 8 small cakes and dust lightly with flour. Place in the refrigerator to chill for about 1 hour. Heat the remaining oil and butter in a large pan and fry the cakes for 4–5 minutes on each side, until golden and slightly crisp. Serve topped with the mustard butter, cut into slices 1/2-inch thick.

Red Pepper Spaetzle with Melting Gruyère

2 red peppers
1 large red chile
1/4 cup olive oil
1 1/2 cups all purpose flour
1/4 teaspoon baking powder
2 eggs
Freshly grated nutmeg
**1/2 cup grated Gruyère cheese or
    Swiss cheese**
Salt and freshly ground black pepper

These delicate Austrian noodles-cum-dumplings make a refreshing change from rice or pasta as an accompaniment. They are usually quite plain but my recipe includes roasted pepper purée to give an eye-catching dish.

Preheat the oven to 350°F. Place the peppers and chile in a baking dish, spoon over 2 tablespoons of the oil and roast for 40 minutes, until soft and lightly charred. Remove from the oven and place in a bowl, cover with plastic wrap and leave for 5 minutes. Peel and seed, then place in a blender and blitz to a smooth purée.

Sift the flour and baking powder into a bowl. Beat in the eggs, then add the red pepper purée. Season with salt, pepper and nutmeg.

Bring a large pot of salted water to a boil. Rest a colander over the pot, ensuring that it does not touch the water. Pour a little of the batter into the colander and press through the holes into the boiling water using a spatula. When the spaetzle float to the surface, cover the pot until they are swollen and fluffy, about 3–4 minutes. Remove the spaetzle with a slotted spoon and dunk into iced water to refresh them. Drain well, then leave to dry on a cloth. Repeat until all the batter has been used.

To serve, heat the remaining oil in a large frying pan, add the spaetzle and toss them in the oil until heated through and lightly golden. Season with salt, pepper and nutmeg and transfer to a serving dish. Sprinkle the Gruyère over them and place under a hot broiler until the cheese begins to melt. Serve immediately.

PG TIPS The spaetzle can be prepared a day in advance, then kept in the fridge on a tray covered with a damp cloth. Reheat them in the oil and top with the cheese just before serving.

'an interesting alternative to rice and noodles, topped with lashings of melted cheese'

Stuffed Artichoke Rösti
with Brie, Bacon and Cumin

2 large potatoes

3 tablespoons unsalted butter

1 small onion, finely chopped

1/2 teaspoon cumin seeds

3 oz. piece of smoked slab bacon (or, if unavailable, around 10 strips of bacon), cut into lardons (short strips)

9 oz. Jerusalem artichokes

Freshly grated nutmeg

1/4 lb. Brie, rind removed, sliced

Salt and freshly ground black pepper

Rösti is a Swiss grated potato cake fried in butter. My recipe goes one stage further, mixing Jerusalem artichokes, bacon and cumin into the potatoes and filling the cake with cheese. It makes a great accompaniment to poultry or meat dishes.

Boil the potatoes in their skins until just tender, about 20 minutes. Drain well and peel while they are still warm.

Heat 1 tablespoon of the butter in a small pan, add the onion and cumin seeds and cook over a gentle heat until the onion is softened but not browned. Raise the heat, add the lardons and fry for 2 minutes.

Grate the potatoes into a bowl, then stir in the onion and bacon mixture. Peel the artichokes and grate them coarsely into the bowl. Mix well together, then season with salt, pepper and nutmeg.

Heat the remaining butter in an 8-inch non-stick frying pan until foaming. Add half the potato and artichoke mixture and press down with a spatula or the back of a spoon to compact it. Cook for about 5–8 minutes, until golden brown underneath, then arrange the sliced cheese on top, leaving a 3/4-inch border. Season, then top with the remaining potato mixture, pressing it down again.

Carefully turn the potato cake over (if you find this tricky, slide it on to a plate, invert the pan on top and then flip it over). Cook on the second side until golden brown and cooked through, about 8–10 minutes.

PG TIPS When cutting lardons, place the piece of bacon in the freezer for up to 3 hours first to make it easier to slice.

'cut open the potato cake to reveal an oozing blend of soft cheese and smoky bacon'

cabbage family

Cabbages are hardly the most glamorous of vegetables. At best, they seem worthy but dull; at worst – boiled to death, like the infamous school-dinners cabbage – they are coarse, sulphurous and indigestible. Yet there's more to the ancient and plentiful brassica family than meets the eye. Cabbages have been cultivated at least since Roman times and are astonishingly diverse: from the smooth, pale common or Dutch cabbage to the handsome, ruffled Savoy, crisp, curly-leaved kale, tiny Brussels sprouts and beautiful, burnished red cabbage. Then there are the exotic cousins from the Far East: pale-stemmed pak choi, crisp and delicate Chinese cabbage and the pretty, flowering choi sum and

Kohlrabi (left)

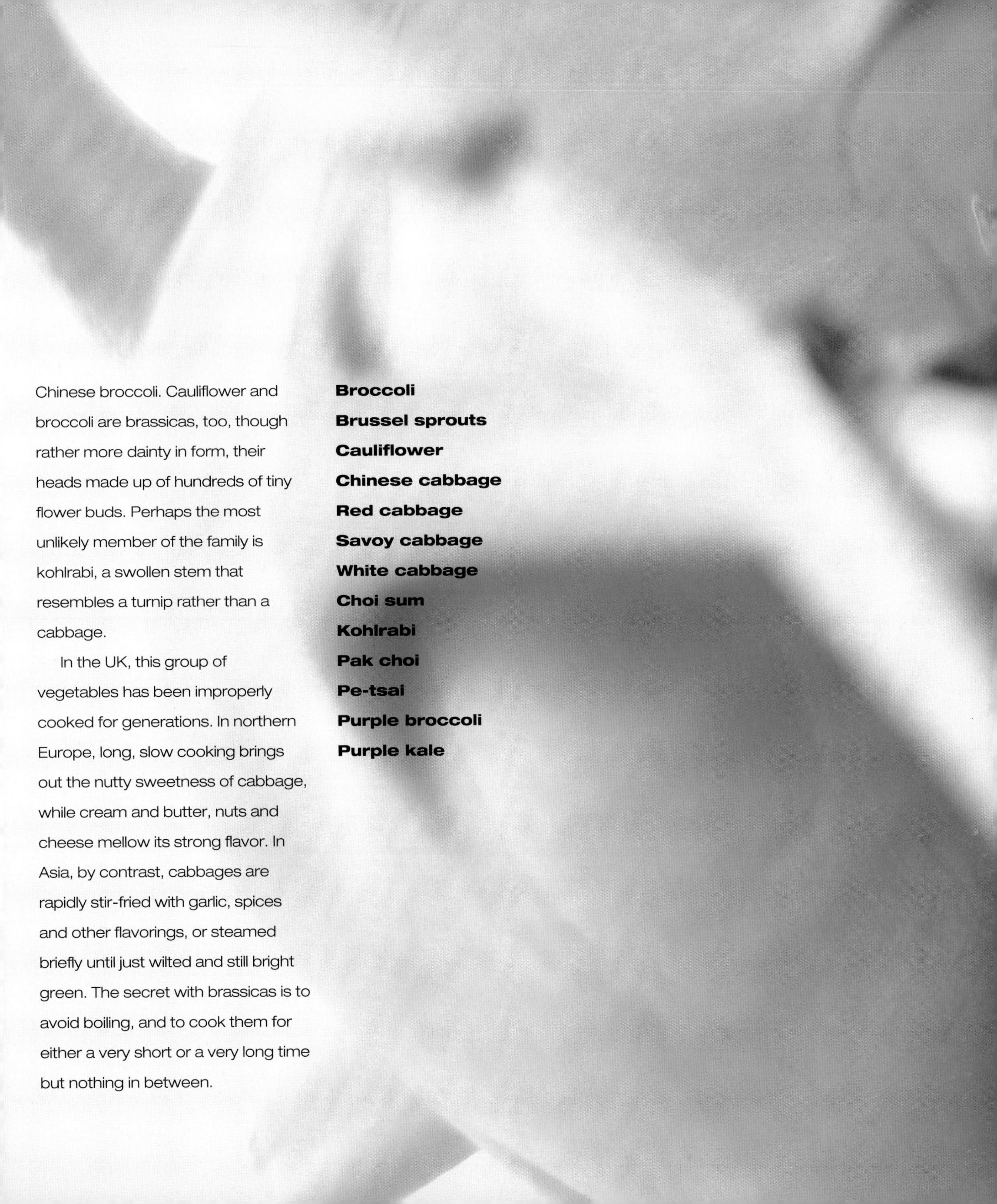

Chinese broccoli. Cauliflower and broccoli are brassicas, too, though rather more dainty in form, their heads made up of hundreds of tiny flower buds. Perhaps the most unlikely member of the family is kohlrabi, a swollen stem that resembles a turnip rather than a cabbage.

In the UK, this group of vegetables has been improperly cooked for generations. In northern Europe, long, slow cooking brings out the nutty sweetness of cabbage, while cream and butter, nuts and cheese mellow its strong flavor. In Asia, by contrast, cabbages are rapidly stir-fried with garlic, spices and other flavorings, or steamed briefly until just wilted and still bright green. The secret with brassicas is to avoid boiling, and to cook them for either a very short or a very long time but nothing in between.

Broccoli

Brussel sprouts

Cauliflower

Chinese cabbage

Red cabbage

Savoy cabbage

White cabbage

Choi sum

Kohlrabi

Pak choi

Pe-tsai

Purple broccoli

Purple kale

Simple Minted Summer Peas

1½ lbs. small young peas in
   their pods
¾ stick (⅓ cup) unsalted butter,
   softened
3 Romaine or Little Gem lettuce
   hearts, shredded
4 scallions, cut into 3 in. lengths
3 sprigs of fresh mint, plus 1
   tablespoon chopped fresh mint
2 cups water
1 teaspoon sugar
Salt and freshly ground black pepper

A delicious recipe for the first of the summer peas, served in their cooking juices with fresh mint. This recipe is adopted from a late-eighteenth-century one and I think it is still one of the nicest ways to serve this delicate vegetable.

Shell the peas and place in a saucepan with the butter, lettuce, scallions, mint sprigs and water. Season with salt and pepper and add the sugar. Bring to a boil and simmer gently for about 15–20 minutes, until the peas are tender. Remove the mint sprigs and add the chopped mint in their place. Serve the peas in the buttery minted juices.

Twice-cooked Belgian endive
with the Flavors of Provence

4 large, plump white Belgian endive
   heads
2 tablespoons unsalted butter
2 teaspoons sugar
Juice of ½ lemon
⅔ cup water
3 tablespoons olive oil
2 garlic cloves, crushed
1 teaspoon fresh thyme leaves
2 teaspoons tomato paste
¾ lb. plum tomatoes, skinned,
   seeded and coarsely chopped
12 black olives
1 small bay leaf
2 tablespoons coarsely chopped
   fresh basil leaves
Salt and freshly ground black pepper

Belgian endive is very much underused. People tend to save it for salads, but it is excellent when cooked. Here it is braised and then baked in a rich tomato sauce.

Preheat the oven to 400°F. Remove any bruised or marked outer leaves from the endive and take out the core with a small knife. Take a shallow casserole dish, just big enough to hold the endive in a single layer, and grease it liberally with the butter. Place the endive in it, sprinkle over it half the sugar and a pinch of salt, then the lemon juice and water. Cover first with a piece of foil, then a heat-resistant plate big enough to fit on top of the endive, inside the casserole, and finally with a tight-fitting lid. Bake for about 45 minutes or until the endive is just tender. Remove the endive from the casserole dish and drain well.

   For the sauce, heat the oil in a pan with the garlic, add the thyme and cook for 1 minute. Add the tomato paste and cook for 5 minutes. Stir in the chopped tomatoes and the remaining sugar, plus the olives and bay leaf and leave to bubble down steadily until thickish and moist in consistency, about 10 minutes. Season to taste, add the basil and stir well.

   Place the endive in a shallow baking dish, pour the sauce over, and return to the oven for about 10–12 minutes, until lightly colored.

Braised Celery
with Meat Marrow and Gruyère

1 large head of celery
³/₄ stick (¹/₃ cup) unsalted butter
1 small onion, finely diced
1 carrot, finely diced
2¹/₂ cups meat stock
¹/₄ cup all purpose flour
5 oz. meat marrow (removed
** from the bone), cut into thick slices**
¹/₂ cup grated Gruyère cheese or
** Swiss cheese**

At the time of writing it is not possible to buy meat marrow in the UK, but hopefully in the not-too-distant future it will be available again… Celery is a surprisingly versatile vegetable with a mild but distinctive flavor. Braising it produces delicious natural juices, which form the base for the sauce in this dish.

Preheat the oven to 375°F. Peel off coarse strings from the celery, then cut off the leaves and set aside.

Melt 2 tablespoons of the butter in a casserole dish over a moderate heat. Add the onion, carrot and celery leaves and sweat for 8–10 minutes, until tender and lightly golden.

Meanwhile, bring a pot of boiling salted water to a boil. Cut the celery stalks into 5-inch lengths and blanch for 5 minutes, then remove and drain well. Place the celery on top of the softened vegetables and pour the meat stock over. Bring to a boil, then reduce the heat, cover and place in the oven to braise for up to 1 hour, until tender. Remove the celery with a slotted spoon. Strain the stock.

Heat the remaining butter in a pan, add the flour and stir well to blend. Gradually add the cooking liquid from the celery, then bring to a boil, stirring. Simmer for 10–15 minutes, then strain through a fine sieve.

Arrange the cooked celery in a gratin dish, top with the slices of meat marrow, then pour the sauce on top. Sprinkle with the Gruyère and return to the oven for 10–15 minutes, until the cheese melts.

PG TIPS An old-fashioned butcher's shop should be able to sell you bone marrow and may even remove it from the bones for you. If you have to do this yourself, however, ask for the bones to be cut into 3-inch lengths and then poach them for 1–2 minutes so you can scoop out the marrow easily.

'caramelizing
young
beets brings
out the
vegetable's
natural
sweetness'

Braised Beets with Shallots

**1 lb. 2 oz. small to medium
   beets**
²/₃ cup red wine
2 tablespoons red wine vinegar
2 tablespoons sugar
**1¹/₄ cups well-flavored vegetable
   stock**
**9 oz. small shallots, blanched
   and peeled (around 10-12)**
Salt and freshly ground black pepper

This is the first dish I ever cooked in a professional kitchen. It was the chef's vegetarian special of the day, 100 portions to be ready for lunch – a little daunting for a young lad new to the business. It still remains a firm favorite of mine. The red wine and sugar form a delicious sweet and sour glaze around the beets.

Preheat the oven to 375°F. Peel the beets carefully, retaining their shape, then cut them into slices ¹/₂-inch thick and set aside.

Put the red wine, vinegar, sugar and vegetable stock in a pan and bring to a boil. Arrange the beets and shallots in a single layer in an ovenproof dish. Pour the red wine mixture over them and season with salt and pepper. Cover with foil or a tight-fitting lid and bake for about 1–1¹/₄ hours or until the vegetables are tender. Serve immediately.

PG TIPS For a nice variation, top the beets with a spoonful of creamed horseradish before serving. I often serve this with grilled meat such as calf's liver or veal.

Braised Fennel
with Sour Orange and Chestnuts

**4 fennel bulbs, trimmed and cut into
   quarters**
³/₄ stick (¹/₃ cup) unsalted butter
¹/₂ teaspoon sugar
**3 oz. vacuum-packed chestnuts
   (around a heaped ¹/₂ cup)**
Zest of 1 Seville orange
Juice of 3 Seville oranges
Juice of 1 lemon
1 teaspoon ground star anise
Salt and freshly ground black pepper

A light medley of winter fennel and chestnuts, enhanced with a spiced orange glaze. This combination is something I like to serve with veal or with game birds such as partridge or pheasant when in season.

Cook the fennel in boiling salted water for 15 minutes, then drain and leave to cool.

Heat the butter in a shallow pan. When it begins to color, add the fennel. Sprinkle with the sugar and leave to caramelize for 8–10 minutes. When golden, add the chestnuts and let them caramelize with the fennel.

Add the orange zest and juice, lemon juice and ground star anise and boil until the liquid has reduced enough to form a syrup around the vegetables. Season to taste and serve immediately.

Braised Stuffed Belgian endive

4 white Belgian endive heads

3/4 stick (1/3 cup) butter

1 teaspoon sugar

2/3 cup water

Juice of 1/2 lemon

6 oz. bulk pork sausage

3 oz. vacuum-packed chestnuts, finely chopped (a slightly-heaped 1/2 cup)

1/4 cup fresh white breadcrumbs

2 tablespoons chopped fresh parsley

8 thin slices of cooked ham

5 tablespoons dry white wine

1/2 cup heavy cream

1/4 cup grated Gruyère cheese or Swiss cheese

Salt and freshly ground black pepper

Preheat the oven to 400°F. Remove any bruised or marked outer leaves from the endive and take out the core with a small knife. Liberally grease a shallow casserole dish with 2 tablespoons of the butter, arrange the endive in it in a single layer and sprinkle over it the sugar and a pinch of salt, then the water and lemon juice. Cover first with a piece of foil then a heat-resistant plate that just fits inside the casserole dish, and finally with a tight-fitting lid. Bake until tender, about 30–35 minutes. Drain well and leave to cool.

In a bowl combine the bulk sausage, chestnuts, breadcrumbs and parsley and season well. Gently squeeze out any excess liquid from the endive and cut each one in half lengthways. Carefully remove a few of the small inner leaves, then stuff the cavities with the filling and fold over the endive to secure.

In a frying pan large enough to hold the endive in a single layer, heat half the remaining butter until foaming. Add the endive and fry until lightly golden. Wrap each endive in a slice of ham and arrange in a gratin dish. Pour the wine and cream over it and finally sprinkle the cheese on top. Dot with the remaining butter, return to the oven and cook for 40 minutes. Serve hot and bubbling from the oven.

PG TIPS Walnuts can be used instead of chestnuts.

Boozy Carrots (Braised in Madeira)

I lb. carrots, sliced into rounds 1/4 in. thick

1/2 stick (1/4 cup) unsalted butter, cut into small nuggets

1 teaspoon sugar

5 tablespoons Madeira (preferably Bual)

1 bottle of still Vichy water (or other bottled water)

Salt and freshly ground black pepper

This is a variation of the classic French Vichy carrots, which are cooked in Vichy mineral water. The Madeira gives them a delicious syrupy glaze.

Place the carrots in a shallow saucepan, top with the butter and sprinkle the sugar on top. Season lightly with salt and pepper. Add the Madeira and enough Vichy water just to cover the carrots. Cover the surface with a piece of buttered wax paper and then cover the pan with a lid.

Cook over a fairly high heat, shaking the carrots occasionally (do not stir them), for 10–15 minutes or until they are tender and coated in the glossy Madeira glaze.

Slow-cooked Leeks in Burgundy Wine

¹/₂ stick (¹/₄ cup) unsalted butter
1¹/₄ lbs. medium-sized leeks,
  cut into 3 in. lengths
1 bottle of Burgundy (or other red
  wine)
1 sprig of fresh thyme
¹/₂ bay leaf
Freshly grated nutmeg
Salt and freshly ground black pepper

Cooking the leeks slowly allows the flavors to develop.

Melt the butter in a heavy saucepan, add the leeks, then cover and sweat without letting them brown. Pour in the red wine, add the thyme and bay leaf and season lightly with salt, pepper and nutmeg. Bring to a boil, then lower the heat, cover and cook for about 1–1¹/₂ hours, until the leeks are tender. Alternatively cook in a moderate oven for 2 hours.

PG TIPS I am a great believer in never throwing anything away. The tougher green parts of the leek may be used when making stocks, sauces or soups.

Stout-braised Winter Vegetables

2 tablespoons virgin olive oil

3/4 lb. small onions (about 1–1 1/4 in. in
   diameter), blanched and peeled

4 celery stalks, cut into 2 in. batons

2 garlic cloves, crushed

6 oz. young carrots, scraped

2/3 cup stout (or other dark
   beer)

1/2 cup tomato juice

1 cup vegetable stock

1 tablespoon brown sugar

Salt and freshly ground black pepper

Beer is a wonderful ingredient – ask any chef! When used in cooking it adds an extra dimension to vegetables, especially roots, as it counteracts their natural sugars. Don't stop with the vegetables used here – try parsnips, rutabaga and turnips as well.

Heat the olive oil in a large pan, add the onions and celery and fry over a moderate heat until lightly golden, about 10–12 minutes. Add the garlic and cook for a couple of minutes, then stir in the carrots. Add the beer, tomato juice, vegetable stock and sugar and bring to a boil. Cover the pan, reduce the heat and cook gently for about 10 minutes or until the vegetables are tender.

Arrange the vegetables in a serving dish, then season the sauce and pour it over them. It should be thick enough to glaze the vegetables; if necessary, boil it down a little first to thicken it.

'the sweet
and sour
flavors
of winter
vegetables
braised with
beer'

'the vibrant
colors of red
cabbage and
dried fruits
evoke
memories
of family
Christmases'

Flemish-style Red Cabbage with Dried Fruits and Juniper

1¹/₂ lbs. red cabbage, core
   removed, finely shredded
1¹/₄ cups red wine
²/₃ cup port
5 tablespoons red wine vinegar
1 tablespoon brown sugar
2¹/₂ cups well-flavored chicken
   stock
1 cup mixed ready-to-eat dried
   fruits, such as apricot, pear, fig
   and apple, halved
12 juniper berries
2 tablespoons redcurrant jelly
Salt and freshly ground black pepper

I adore braised red cabbage and cannot understand why it is so often only cooked around Christmas time. It deserves to be savored more widely. This combination of red cabbage, dried fruits and juniper is particularly good. It makes the perfect accompaniment to roast pork and many game dishes.

Preheat the oven to 400°F. Place the shredded cabbage in a large ovenproof dish, pour over it the red wine, port and wine vinegar, then sprinkle on the sugar and season lightly.

Bring the stock to a boil, then pour it over the cabbage and add the dried fruit and juniper berries. Bring to a boil, cover with a tight-fitting lid, then transfer to the oven and braise for up to 1 hour or until the cabbage is very tender. If any liquid remains, uncover the pan and continute to cook until evaporated. Add the redcurrant jelly, mix well to form a glaze around the cabbage, then serve immediately.

PG TIPS Braised red cabbage is an ideal dish for reheating the next day; in fact it improves the flavor.

Wilted Greens with Chili Oil

1¹/₄ lbs. mixed bitter greens,
   such as curly kale, Swiss chard,
   mustard greens and turnip greens
¹/₄ cup olive oil
1¹/₂ teaspoons chili oil
1 garlic clove, crushed
1 tablespoon sweet chili sauce
1 teaspoon ketjap manis (Indonesian
   soy sauce)
¹/₂ cup water
Salt and freshly ground black pepper

If you are looking for a dish with a little spring in its step, look no further. The chili oil and sweet chili sauce complement the buttery greens magnificently to form a simple Asian treat.

Shred the greens coarsely, removing any central cores as you go. Heat the olive oil and chili oil in a wok, add the garlic and sauté for 30 seconds. Add the greens and toss for 4–5 minutes until they are coated with the oil. Add the chili sauce, ketjap manis and water. Cover with a lid and steam the greens for 1 minute, then season and serve.

PG TIPS You can cook any sturdy greens this way, although remember that cooking times will vary. Spinach, for example, wilts in a minute or two.

Wok-fried Choi Sum
with Shiitake and Tamari

1 lb. choi sum (Chinese flowering cabbage)
2 tablespoons peanut oil
1 garlic clove, crushed
1 tablespoon finely chopped fresh ginger
a heaped cup shiitake mushrooms
1/2 cup fresh or canned Chinese water chestnuts, peeled and thinly sliced
1/2 cup chicken stock
2 tablespoons cornstarch
2 tablespoons tamari (or dark soy sauce)
1 tablespoon sesame oil
1 tablespoon roasted peanuts

Oriental-style greens are much more commonplace than they used to be, thanks to the growth of interest in Thai and Chinese cooking. All the ingredients for this dish are now readily available – so get to wok!

Separate the stems from the leaves of the choi sum and cut them into pieces 2-inches long. Blanch the stems in boiling salted water until just tender, then drain well.

Heat a wok or deep frying pan, add the peanut oil, garlic, ginger, choi sum stems, mushrooms and water chestnuts and stir-fry for 3–4 minutes. Add the choi sum leaves and cook for a minute longer.

Blend the stock with the cornstarch to form a paste and stir it into the pan. Stir in the tamari and sesame oil and toss well together. The sauce should form a glaze around the vegetables. Sprinkle the peanuts over them and serve immediately

Wok-seared Sugarsnaps
with Anise and Mint

2 tablespoons peanut oil
14 oz. sugarsnap peas (2 very large handfuls)
1 green chile, seeded and finely chopped
1 small lemongrass stalk, finely chopped
1 garlic clove, crushed
1/2 teaspoon finely chopped fresh ginger
A pinch each of ground coriander, cumin and star anise
2 tablespoons nam pla (Thai fish sauce)
1/2 cup coconut milk
1 tablespoon chopped fresh mint

This is seasoned with nam pla, a thin brown sauce made from salted, fermented fish. When it is cooked, some of the fishy taste is diminished, leaving a pleasant but distinct flavor.

Heat the oil in a wok or frying pan until very hot. Add the sugarsnaps and chile and stir-fry over a high heat for about 2–3 minutes, until they begin to brown. Add the lemongrass, garlic, ginger and spices and fry for a further 30 seconds. Add the nam pla and coconut milk and cook for a final minute. Pour into a deep serving bowl, sprinkle with the mint and serve immediately.

'roasted
peanuts add
a robust and
juicy crunch
to delicate
oriental
vegetables'

'new potatoes,
warm and
sexy, enriched
with saffron'

Saffron-braised Potatoes with Paprika

1/4 cup olive oil

1 1/2 lbs. new potatoes, lightly scraped

3 garlic cloves, crushed

1 tablespoon tomato paste (or passata)

1 tablespoon coriander seeds

1/2 teaspoon hot Spanish paprika

A good pinch of saffron strands

3 cups well-flavored boiling chicken stock

1 tablespoon chopped fresh coriander leaves

Salt

This is something I came upon by accident when I was asked to create an exciting potato dish for a private function at the Lanesborough. After browsing through a Spanish cookbook a friend had sent me the night before, this was the result.

Heat the olive oil in a wide pot with a lid. Add the potatoes and sauté for 2–3 minutes without letting them color. Add the garlic and cook for a minute longer, then stir in the tomato paste, coriander seeds, paprika and saffron. Add a little salt, then pour in the boiling stock, cover and simmer for 30 minutes, until the potatoes are tender. Raise the heat and boil until the liquid has reduced to a thick sauce, turning the potatoes occasionally. Sprinkle with the coriander leaves and serve hot. It can also be served cold as a first course or salad.

Lemongrass-glazed Carrots and Pink Radishes

3/4 lb. small young carrots with tops, scrubbed

5 oz. young red radishes with tops (around 10-11 radishes)

1/2 stick (1/4 cup) unsalted butter, cut into small pieces

Juice and zest of 1 lemon

1 lemongrass stalk, very finely chopped

1 tablespoon corn syrup or maple syrup

Salt and freshly ground black pepper

Lemon-scented carrots and radishes are a winning combination. When I worked in France, radishes were often cooked to accompany meat dishes but in the UK we almost always serve them raw, in salads or as crudités. For this dish, try to find small, young radishes, as large ones can be quite hot.

Place the carrots and radishes in a pan, add the butter, lemon juice and zest, then sprinkle in the lemongrass and drizzle over the syrup. Add just enough water to cover. Place a circle of buttered wax paper on top and bring to a boil. Reduce the heat slightly and cook until the carrots are tender and the cooking juices form a glaze around the vegetables. Toss well, then season and serve.

PG TIPS Radishes and young carrots are often sold with plenty of healthy green leaves still attached. These leaves have a delicate flavor which gives a fresh kick to soups. Remember, though, to cook them only briefly in the soup, otherwise their flavor and color will be dulled.

Crisp Cauliflower and Broccoli with Walnut-fried Rice

2 tablespoons sesame oil
1 tablespoon unsalted butter
1 small cauliflower, divided into small
 flowerets
1 small head of broccoli, divided into
 small flowerets
1 garlic clove, crushed
1/2 in. piece of fresh ginger,
 grated
a generous 1/2 cup cooked basmati
 rice
1/4 cup walnuts, finely chopped
1/4 cup oyster sauce
1/2 cup vegetable or chicken
 stock
Salt and freshly ground black pepper

Walnut-flavored rice makes a nice change with crisp cauliflower and broccoli flowerets. Oyster sauce completes the light oriental touch.

Heat the sesame oil and butter in a wok until smoking, add the cauliflower, broccoli, garlic and ginger and stir-fry for 1 minute. Add the rice and walnuts and sauté for 2–3 minutes. Season to taste. Transfer to a serving dish and keep warm.

Clean the wok with a wad of paper towels and place back on the heat. Add the oyster sauce and stock and boil for 2 minutes. Pour it over the cauliflower and broccoli and serve immediately.

Baked Pumpkin with Chile, Lime and Soy

3/4 stick (1/3 cup) unsalted butter
11/2 lbs. pumpkin, peeled,
 seeded and cut into slices 1/4 in.
 thick
1 red chile, thinly sliced
2 tablespoons light soy sauce
Juice of 1 lime
2 in. piece of fresh ginger, finely
 grated
1 teaspoon light molasses
2 garlic cloves, crushed
About 2 cups boiling chicken
 stock
Salt and freshly ground black pepper

Although pumpkin is not much used in Asian cooking, I find oriental spices work very well with it. Other types of squash such as butternut could be used instead.

Preheat the oven to 375°F. Use 2 tablespoons of the butter to grease a gratin dish, then arrange the pumpkin slices attractively in it in layers, seasoning each layer with salt and pepper.

Melt the remaining butter in a pan and stir in the chile, soy sauce, lime juice and ginger, then the molasses and garlic. Pour this mixture over the pumpkin.

Pour in enough boiling chicken stock just to cover the pumpkin, then place in the oven and bake for about 40–50 minutes or until the pumpkin is tender.

Fufu (Crushed Sweet Potatoes with Bacon and Onion)

4 large orange-fleshed sweet
   potatoes, well scrubbed
1/4 cup, plus 2 tablespoons olive oil
1/4 lb. bacon (around 8-10 strips),
   chopped
1 red onion, finely chopped
1 tablespoon jerk seasoning
1/4 cup fresh white breadcrumbs
2 tablespoons chopped fresh parsley
1 tablespoon chopped fresh
   coriander leaves
2 tablespoons unsalted butter,
   melted
Salt and freshly ground black pepper

Fufu, or foo-foo, comes from the Caribbean and is a dish of pounded plaintain or ground rice, although I have also seen it made with sweet potatoes and even cassava. I prefer a coarser version, spiced with jerk seasoning and served in vegetable shells – a more sophisticated presentation!

Preheat the oven to 350°F. Prick the sweet potatoes with a small knife, then rub them with 1/4 cup of the oil. Place on a baking sheet and bake for 1 hour or until tender. Remove and leave until cool enough to handle. Cut a slice off the top of each potato and scoop out the flesh into a bowl, leaving the shell intact. Crush the potato flesh coarsely with a fork.

Heat the remaining oil in a frying pan, add the bacon and fry for 5 minutes, until crisp. Add the onion and fry for 2–3 minutes. Stir in the potato flesh and season with the jerk seasoning, salt and pepper.

Fill the potato shells with the fufu. Mix the breadcrumbs with the parsley and coriander leaves. Pour the melted butter over the potatoes and scatter the herb breadcrumbs on top. Place in the oven for 10 minutes to form a golden crust.

PG TIPS Jerking is a Jamaican cooking method that involves marinating meat or chicken in a thick paste of allspice, chili, pepper, bay leaf, sugar and Worcestershire sauce. A bottled version of jerk seasoning is available in West Indian shops and is well worth seeking out.

Sugar-roasted Pumpkin
with Cardamom Butter and Toasted Pepitas

1 lb., 10 oz. pumpkin, peeled and
    cut into wedges
2 tablespoons vegetable oil
2 tablespoons unsalted butter
Zest of 1 orange
1/2 teaspoon cardamom pods,
    cracked to release the seeds
1 tablespoon pumpkin seeds, toasted
Salt and freshly ground black pepper

The only sugar in this recipe is the natural sugar in the pumpkin itself, which forms a light caramel during roasting. When the pumpkin is topped with the spicy butter, flavors explode!

Preheat the oven to 350°F. Place the pumpkin in a roasting pan, season with salt and pepper and toss with the oil. Roast until tender and lightly caramelized, about 40 minutes.

    Heat the butter, orange zest and cardamom seeds in a small pan until the butter has melted and then pour it over the pumpkin. Toss to coat with the butter and roast for 10 minutes. Transfer to a serving dish, spoon over it the pan juices and serve immediately, topped with the toasted pumpkin seeds.

P.G. TIPS It's easier to use bought pumpkin seeds (also called pepitas) than the ones from the pumpkin, since they are usually too wet to toast.

Dry-roasted Corn with Smoked Garlic
and Parsley Butter

4 corn on the cob
3 tablespoons olive oil
Salt and freshly ground black pepper

For the butter:
4 smoked garlic cloves, crushed
1 stick (1/2 cup) unsalted butter
1 tablespoon chopped fresh parsley

Corn is the only grain native to America. There are hundreds of traditional American recipes for it, such as Succotash (see page 60) and Hush Puppies (see page 100).

Preheat the oven to 375°F. Soak the unhusked corn cobs in hand-hot water for 30 minutes, then drain thoroughly. Tear off all but the last 2 layers of husk and brush with the oil. Place in a shallow baking tray and roast for 45 minutes–1 hour, brushing with more oil if necessary and turning occasionally.

    Meanwhile, prepare the butter by beating all the ingredients together in a bowl. Season to taste.

    Serve the corn hot from the oven: just pull back the husks and top with the garlic butter.

PG TIPS You'll never believe that something so tasty could be produced from so few ingredients. The garlic butter is a revelation. It's worth making double the amount and freezing it. Try it tossed with pasta or sautéed with mushrooms. If you can't find smoked garlic, normal can be substituted.

'a charred
smokiness
gives this
pumpkin dish
its wonderful
flavor'

Gingerbread-spiced Parsnips

1 lb. parsnips, peeled, cores
removed if large, and cut into
coarse chunks

2¹/₂ cups well-flavored chicken
stock

¹/₂ stick (¹/₄ cup) unsalted butter

¹/₂ in. piece of fresh ginger,
finely chopped

¹/₄ teaspoon ground cinnamon

¹/₄ teaspoon ground coriander

¹/₃ cup finely chopped almonds

5 oz. gingerbread, finely
crumbled (to yield 1²/₃ cups)

1 tablespoon chopped fresh
coriander leaves

Salt and freshly ground black pepper

The idea of mixing tender vegetables with crisp golden breadcrumbs is nothing new but how about using gingerbread instead? It adds a superb, spicy-sweet flavor to the parsnips. Be sure to use a fairly dry Continental-style gingerbread rather than a sticky ginger cake.

Place the parsnips in a pan, pour in the chicken stock and bring to a boil. Reduce the heat to a simmer and cook for 15 minutes or until tender. Drain and keep warm.

Heat the butter in a pan, add the ginger, cinnamon, ground coriander and nibbed almonds and fry for 2 minutes. Stir in the gingerbread and fresh coriander leaves. Add the cooked parsnips and toss gently together, then season to taste and serve.

PG TIPS I sometimes top the parsnips with a little Parmesan cheese.

Turnip, Oven-dried Tomato and Thyme Dauphinois

1 tablespoon unsalted butter

1 lb., 2 oz. turnips, thinly sliced

¹/₄ lb. oven-dried tomatoes (see
Tips below), roughly chopped

1¹/₂ cups heavy cream

²/₃ cup milk

1 garlic clove, crushed

1 tablespoon fresh thyme leaves

¹/₂ cup mascarpone cheese

¹/₂ cup grated Cheddar cheese

Salt and freshly ground black pepper

Preheat the oven to 350°F. Use the butter to grease a 10-inch gratin dish. Arrange the turnips overlapping in layers in the dish, interspersed with the oven-dried tomatoes and seasoning between the layers with just a little salt – the tomatoes can be quite salty. Arrange the final layer neatly, using both turnips and tomatoes.

Bring the cream, milk, garlic and thyme to a boil, then remove from the heat and stir in the mascarpone. Pour through a strainer on to the turnips, ensuring the liquid covers them. Sprinkle with the cheese and bake for 40–45 minutes or until the turnips are tender and the top is golden and crusty.

PG TIPS To prepare oven-dried tomatoes, take 1 lb. ripe plum tomatoes, cut them in half lengthwise and place, cut-side up, on a wire rack over a baking tray. Sprinkle with a little salt, pepper and sugar, drizzle over a little olive oil and leave for an hour. Transfer to a baking sheet and bake in an oven preheated to 375°F for 1 hour. Leave to cool before using.

Tunisian Carrot Salad

1 lb. young carrots, scraped
2 garlic cloves, thinly sliced
$1/2$ teaspoon coriander seeds
$1/4$ teaspoon dried chili flakes
1 cup green olives in brine,
  drained
1 teaspoon cumin seeds, toasted
2 tablespoons lemon juice
2 tablespoons orange juice
Zest of $1/2$ orange
$1/2$ cup olive oil
2 tablespoons coriander leaves
Salt and freshly ground black pepper

If I had a pound for every recipe for carrot salads from the Mediterranean I have seen I would be a rich man. They are combined with honey, raisins, nuts and all manner of spices and herbs. In my version they are mixed with a spicy citrus dressing to make an appealing salad for a picnic or a spring lunch.

Place the whole carrots in a pan with the garlic, coriander seeds and chili flakes and just cover with water. Bring to a boil, reduce the heat and cook until the carrots are just tender but still crisp and the liquid has evaporated. Transfer to a bowl and cool slightly.

Mix together the olives, cumin seeds, lemon juice, orange juice and zest and the oil. Pour this dressing over the carrots and season to taste, then garnish with the coriander leaves and serve warm.

Caramelized Belgian endive with Morels

4 large, plump white Belgian endive
  heads
$1/2$ stick ($1/4$ cup) unsalted butter
4 teaspoons sugar
Juice of $1/2$ lemon
$2/3$ cup water
2 shallots, finely chopped
5 oz. small fresh morel
  mushrooms, cleaned (see page
  172)
$1/4$ lb. piece of slab bacon,
  cut into lardons (see tip page 112)
$1^{1}/4$ cups meat stock
1 tablespoon fresh sage leaves
Salt and freshly ground black pepper

Although I am not a great lover of raw Belgian endive, I am very fond of it cooked, which improves the flavor and removes the bitterness.

Preheat the oven to 400°F. Remove any bruised or marked outer leaves from the endive and take out the core with a small knife. Take a shallow casserole dish just big enough to hold the endive in a single layer and grease it liberally with half the butter. Place the endive in it, sprinkle over it 1 teaspoon of the sugar and a pinch of salt, then the lemon juice and water. Cover first with a piece of foil then a heat-resistant plate big enough to fit on top of the endive, inside the casserole, finally with a tight-fitting lid. Bake for about 45 minutes or until the endive is just tender. Remove the endive from the casserole dish and drain well.

Heat the remaining butter in a pan, add the shallots and morels and sauté until tender, about 5–6 minutes. Raise the heat and add the lardons. Cut the cooked endive in half lengthways and add to the pan. Sprinkle over it the remaining sugar and cook until the endive is lightly caramelized. Finally, pour in the stock, add the sage leaves, then reduce the heat to a simmer. Cover and braise for 10–12 minutes, until the sauce has reduced and slightly thickened. Season to taste. Arrange the caramelized endive in a serving dish, pour the sauce over it, and serve.

Roasted Cauliflower Aigre-doux

1/4 cup light olive oil

1 cauliflower, cut into wedges about
   1¹/2 in. thick, keeping the root
   end intact

3/4 stick (¹/3 cup) unsalted butter

5 tablespoons balsamic vinegar

1¹/2 teaspoons sugar

2 tablespoons superfine capers,
   drained and rinsed

1/3 cup golden raisins, soaked in hot
   water for 5 minutes, then drained

1/4 cup water

Salt and freshly ground black pepper

Traditionalists who like their cauliflower smothered in a rich cheese sauce may be surprised to see it roasted. The roasting process seems to bring out a nutty flavor, which makes a winning combination with the sweet and sour caper topping.

Preheat the oven to 400°F. Heat the olive oil in a roasting pan on the stove, add the cauliflower wedges and cook over a moderate to high heat until lightly golden. Transfer to the oven and cook for 25–30 minutes, until golden brown.

Heat the butter in a small frying pan, add the vinegar and sugar and caramelize lightly together. Stir in the capers, raisins and water and heat through, bubbling for a few minutes if necessary to reduce to a glaze. Season with salt and pepper.

Put the cauliflower in a serving dish and pour over it the sweet and sour capers and golden raisins.

P.G. TIPS Capers are available salted or in vinegar. Whichever you choose, it is a good idea to rinse them before use.

Stock-roasted Baby Carrots with Coriander Seeds and Lime

1/2 stick (¹/4 cup) unsalted butter

1 lb. baby carrots with a little
   stalk attached, scraped

1 teaspoon sugar

1¹/4 cup vegetable stock

1¹/2 teaspoons coriander seeds,
   lightly crushed

Juice and zest of 1 lime

Salt and freshly ground black pepper

Preheat the oven to 450°F. Melt the butter in a small casserole dish, add the carrots and fry for 3–5 minutes, until lightly golden. Stir in the sugar and cook until lightly caramelized. Transfer to the oven and cook for 10 minutes. Pour in the stock and scatter the coriander seeds over the carrots, then return to the oven and cook for 8–10 minutes, until the stock has evaporated and the carrots have taken on a beautiful shiny glaze. Add the lime juice and zest and some seasoning, toss together and serve.

Bonfire-roasted New Potatoes

1 lb. new potatoes, well
   washed
4 banana shallots, unpeeled
2 tablespoons olive oil
1 sprig of fresh rosemary, roughly
   chopped
2 tablespoons unsalted butter
Coarse sea salt and freshly ground
   black pepper

I like to cook these aromatic potato parcels in the embers of the bonfire on Guy Fawkes night but they are also very good cooked on a barbecue.

Bring a pot of salted water to a boil, add the potatoes and shallots and reduce the heat to a simmer. Cook for 10–15 minutes, then drain well. Place in a bowl, season with sea salt and black pepper and add the olive oil and rosemary.

Wrap the potatoes and shallots loosely in 2 or 3 layers of thick foil and place amongst the coals of a barbecue or bonfire at medium temperature. Turning the pouch regularly, cook for about 20 minutes or until the potatoes and shallots are tender and the skins somewhat crisp. Open up the parcel and top with the butter, which will melt over the vegetables. Serve immediately.

Roasted Kohlrabi with Pancetta and Garlic and Thyme Dressing

3 garlic cloves
2 tablespoons, plus ¼ cup olive oil
1½ lbs. kohlrabi, peeled and
   cut into 1 in. dice
2 tablespoons vegetable oil
½ stick (¼ cup) unsalted butter
¼ lb. pancetta, cut into lardons –
   around 1 cup
   (see Tips page 112)
1 tablespoon red wine vinegar
1 teaspoon fresh thyme leaves
Salt and freshly ground black pepper

Kohlrabi is the black sheep of the cabbage family, which is a shame as it is very versatile. Try it raw in salads or cooked and puréed with garlic and herbs. Any recipe for turnips would be good made with kohlrabi instead.

Preheat the oven to 425°F. Put the unpeeled garlic cloves in a small dish, pour over them 2 tablespoons of the olive oil and roast for 10 minutes or until very soft. Remove and leave to cool.

Place the kohlrabi in a roasting pan, pour the vegetable oil over them, dot with the butter and season with salt and pepper. Place in the oven and roast for 20–25 minutes, until golden. Add the pancetta, toss together and return to the oven for 10 minutes.

Squeeze the garlic cloves out of their skins. Place in a bowl with the remaining olive oil, the vinegar and the thyme and mix together to break down the garlic to a purée. Season with salt and pepper.

Remove the kohlrabi from the oven, add the dressing to the pan and toss together. Serve immediately.

the onion family

Can there be any country in the world that does not rely upon the onion family as the foundation of its cooking? Alliums are intrinsic to stocks, broths, marinades, soups, sauces and stews everywhere. In the Far East, onion, shallots and garlic are pounded with chiles and ginger to make spice pastes for flavoring meat, fish and vegetables; in Spain and Portugal onions and garlic are cooked slowly with tomatoes to make a sofrito or refogado respectively, then stored to use as the basis of virtually all savory dishes; in America's Deep South, onions, together with carrots and celery, form the famous 'Holy Trinity' that is fried up before adding other ingredients. Not just a flavoring,

Baby Leeks (left)

alliums also play a starring role in dishes as diverse as the onion and leek tarts of France, the onion pickles and chutneys of both the UK and the Middle East, the aïoli and skordalia of Provence and Greece, the bhajis of India and the champ of Northern Ireland.

The allium family are edible lilies – not so surprising if you have ever seen wild garlic, with its slender, oval leaves. The most remarkable thing about this indispensable group of vegetables is the way their flavor varies according to how they are prepared and cooked. Garlic and onions, for example, roasted or braised whole, develop a delicious sweetness that is quite unlike their pungent character when raw. Leeks and shallots have a naturally milder, more refined flavor that is often partnered with delicate ingredients such as butter, eggs and cream.

Recently chefs have taken a fresh look at the onion family: garlic, onions, shallots and leeks may now be deep-fried, chargrilled, roasted, caramelized, used to make tartes Tatin, terrines, breads, confits and savory marmalades. Perhaps the only one that has been overlooked is the scallion, used as a salad ingredient and not much else. In the Far East, however, its delicate texture and mild flavor are exploited in stir-fries and other quick-cooking dishes.

Baby Leeks

Button onions

Onions

Red onions

Pickling onions

Scallions

Garlic

Leeks

Shallots

Slow-roasted Radicchio with Pancetta and Raisins

2 garlic cloves, crushed
1/2 cup olive oil
1 teaspoon fresh thyme leaves
5 tablespoons balsamic vinegar
1/3 cup raisins, soaked in hot
     water for 30 minutes, then drained
     and dried
2 radicchio, core removed, halved
     through the root
8 thin slices of pancetta
2 tablespoons pine nuts, toasted
2 tablespoons freshly grated
     Parmesan cheese
Salt and freshly ground black pepper

This bitter salad leaf is often served cooked in Italy, its home country. Here it is partnered with bacon and sweet raisins.

Mix together the garlic, olive oil, thyme, vinegar and raisins to make a marinade, then season and set aside. Blanch the radicchio in boiling water for 5 minutes or until just tender, then drain well. Add the radicchio to the marinade and toss to coat. Cover with plastic wrap and leave to marinate at room temperature for 2 hours.

   Preheat the oven to 400°F. Remove the radicchio halves from the marinade and wrap each one in 2 pancetta slices. Arrange them in a baking dish, pour the marinade over them, and place in the oven. Roast until the radicchio leaves are crisp and wilted; this will take 45 minutes–1 hour. Serve hot from the oven, sprinkled with pine nuts, Parmesan and remaining cooking juices.

PG TIPS To toast nuts, seeds or spices, place them in a dry heavy-based frying pan over a low heat and cook, stirring frequently, for about 1 minute, until golden – or until fragrant in the case of spices. Alternatively place on a baking sheet and toast in an oven preheated to 350°F for 5–8 minutes.

Kumera with Tequila, Maple and Passionfruit Glaze

1 lb. orange-fleshed sweet
     potatoes, cut into chunks
2 tablespoons vegetable oil
2 tablespoons unsalted butter,
     melted
2 tablespoons maple syrup
2 tablespoons tequila
Juice of 2 passionfruit, strained to
     remove the seeds
1 teaspoon chopped fresh marjoram
2 tablespoons sliced almonds,
     toasted (optional)
Salt and freshly ground black pepper

Ever since I spent a period at the Lanesborough's sister hotel, the Mansion on Turtle Creek in Dallas, I have been partial to a Margarita or two, so much so that I now use tequila occasionally in cooking. It works perfectly with kumera (orange sweet potatoes) and passionfruit.

Preheat the oven to 450°F. Put the sweet potatoes in a roasting pan, season lightly and pour the oil and melted butter over them. Roast for 20–25 minutes, until golden.

   Add the maple syrup, tequila and passionfruit juice, toss lightly and return to the oven until the potatoes have caramelized. Sprinkle over them the marjoram and toss once more. Place in a serving dish and scatter the almonds on top, if using.

Coriander-mashed Potato with Charred Chiles

1 poblano chile
5 tablespoons olive oil
1¹/₂ lbs. potatoes, preferably Russet,
    peeled and cut into chunks
1 garlic clove, crushed
¹/₂ stick (¹/₄ cup) unsalted butter
2 tablespoons chopped fresh
    coriander leaves
Salt and freshly ground black pepper

This is one of the great mash recipes, with all the flavor of the Southwest bursting out. Poblano chiles are one of the most commonly used varieties in Mexican cooking. Roasting the chile intensifies the smoky flavor that makes this dish so special. If you cannot find a poblano, use a large red serrano chile instead.

Preheat a broiler or a ridged grill pan. Put the chile in a bowl and toss with 1 tablespoon of the oil. Broil until charred on all sides, then return it to the bowl and cover with plastic wrap. Leave for 5 minutes, then peel carefully, remove the seeds and chop the chile finely.
  Cook the potatoes in boiling salted water until very tender, then drain well. Strain to give a smooth purée. Beat in the garlic, butter and remaining olive oil. Finally mix in the chopped chile and coriander leaves, season with salt and pepper and serve.

PG TIPS Occasionally I like to top this mash with thinly sliced onions that have been cooked slowly in butter for about 30 minutes until deep golden – great with broiled beef or lamb.

Parsnip and Apple Mash

1 lb., 2 oz. parsnips, chopped,
    central core removed if large
¹/₂ stick (¹/₄ cup) unsalted butter
1 large Cortland or other cooking
    apple (9 oz.), peeled, cored and
    finely chopped
¹/₄ cup heavy cream
¹/₄ cup milk
1 tablespoon creamed horseradish
Salt and freshly ground black pepper

This includes creamed horseradish, which gives the mash a big lift, while the Cortland apples add a touch of acidity to counteract the sweetness of the parsnips.

Cook the parsnips in plenty of boiling salted water until tender, then drain well. Either put the parsnips through a vegetable mill or strain them to obtain a smooth purée.
  Heat half the butter in a pan, add the apples and cook gently until soft and pulpy. Combine the parsnips with the apples and then mix in the cream, milk, horseradish and remaining butter. Season to taste and serve.

PG TIPS If you prepare the parsnips in advance, keep them in a bowl of water containing a slice of lemon to prevent them going brown.

Red Wine and Shallot Mash

1¹/₄ lbs. potatoes (such as
   Russet), scrubbed but not
   peeled
³/₄ stick (¹/₃ cup) unsalted butter
4 shallots, finely chopped
³/₄ cup red wine
5 tablespoons port
¹/₂ cup hot milk
Salt and freshly ground black pepper

Put the potatoes in a large pot, cover with water and bring to a boil. Simmer uncovered over a moderate heat until tender, then drain well.

In a pan heat ¹/₂ tablespoon of the butter (cut the rest into small pieces and chill). Add the shallots to the pan and cook over a low heat for 2–3 minutes. Add the red wine and port and boil until reduced by half its volume.

Peel the potatoes as soon as they are cool enough to handle and pass them through a strainer or vegetable mill. Return them to the pot, add the wine reduction and hot milk and stir vigorously. Add the chilled butter a little at a time, beating as you go, until the mixture is light and fluffy. Reheat gently, season with salt and pepper and serve.

PG TIPS Choosing the right potato is very important. Waxy-fleshed varieties are ideal for cooking methods where you need them to keep their shape, such as boiling, steaming or in salads. Floury potatoes are good for baking, mashing and deep-frying, as they have a fluffier texture when cooked.

Whipped Rutabaga Purée
with Orange Zest and Ginger

2¹/₄ lbs. rutabaga, peeled and cut
   into ¹/₂ in. dice
1 tablespoon grated fresh ginger
2 tablespoons unsalted butter
Juice and zest of 1 orange
5 tablespoons heavy cream
Salt and freshly ground black pepper

This is made in a food processor, which gives a smooth, light, delicate purée.

Put the rutabaga and ginger in a pot, cover with cold water and add a little salt. Bring to a boil and simmer for about 20 minutes, until tender. Leave to drain thoroughly in a colander for several minutes, then transfer to a food processor. Add the butter, orange juice and zest and process for a few seconds. Transfer to a bowl and mix in the cream and some seasoning.

PG TIPS Do not be tempted to mix the heavy cream with the purée in the food processor or it will turn to butter and spoil the dish.

Navy Bean Mash with Walnut Pesto

1 cup navy beans, soaked
   overnight and then drained
1/2 lb. potatoes (preferably Russet),
   peeled and cut into chunks (around
   1 1/2 cups)
1/2 cup virgin olive oil
2 garlic cloves, crushed
Juice of 1/4 lemon
Salt and freshly ground black pepper

For the pesto:
2 oz. (around 1 cup) fresh basil
   leaves
1 garlic clove, crushed
1 tablespoon walnuts
1 tablespoon freshly grated
   Parmesan cheese
A pinch of sugar
6 tablespoons virgin olive oil

This is a variation on brandade, a classic French purée of salt cod and potatoes. My brandade uses creamy white beans instead of fish, enriched with a generous amount of olive oil.

Put the drained beans in a pot, cover with cold water and bring to a boil. Reduce the heat and cook for 1–1 1/2 hours or until very tender, then drain well. Meanwhile, cook the potatoes in boiling salted water until tender, then drain. Purée the beans and potatoes together in a blender or food processor, then gradually add the oil with the motor running. Beat in the garlic, lemon juice and seasoning. Keep warm.

For the pesto, put all the ingredients except the oil in a blender or food processor and blitz for a few seconds until coarsely chopped. Transfer to a bowl. Slowly pour in the oil and blend together. Season to taste.

Put the navy bean mash in a serving bowl, pour the walnut pesto over it, and serve.

PG TIPS Walnut pesto is one of my favorites and appears on my menu regularly. I love to serve it with pasta, wild mushrooms or grilled fish or chicken, or stirred into creamy mashed celeriac or potato.

Button Sprouts with Parmesan and Pearl Onions

3 tablespoons olive oil

20 small pearl onions, blanched and peeled

1 tablespoon light brown sugar

3 tablespoons unsalted butter

1 cup meat stock

3/4 lb. button sprouts (baby Brussels sprouts)

2 tablespoons freshly grated Parmesan cheese

Salt and freshly ground black pepper

At Christmas, Brussels sprouts cooked in boiling water and tossed with butter are enjoyable enough but rather uninspiring. This recipe is a more interesting way of preparing them, combining tiny Brussels with sweet onions and a dusting of fresh Parmesan.

Heat the oil in a frying pan in which the onions will fit in a single layer, add the onions and cook over a high heat until golden all over. Add the sugar and half the butter and cook until the onions are caramelized, about 8–10 minutes. Pour in the stock and cook until it has evaporated.

Meanwhile, cook the Brussels sprouts in boiling salted water until just tender but still retaining a little bite. Drain them well.

In a separate pan, heat the remaining butter until foaming, add the sprouts and sauté for 5 minutes, until golden. Add the onions and toss together, then season with salt and pepper and transfer to a serving dish. Sprinkle with the Parmesan and toss to coat.

PG TIPS Brussels sprouts are a strange vegetable, inspiring either love or hate. I love them, and here are some of my favorite ways of serving them:
• Tossed with roasted chestnuts and celery
• Puréed and finish simply with nutmeg and butter
• Mixed with cream and seasoned with a little curry powder

Potato and Anchovy Aïoli

1 small, floury baking potato (about 4 oz.), such as Russet

3 egg yolks

2/3 cup light olive oil

2 garlic cloves, crushed

4 anchovy fillets, rinsed and finely chopped

Salt and freshly ground black pepper

This is particularly good served with fish, such as fresh tuna burgers or deep-fried or grilled fish.

Bake or boil the potato until tender, then drain and leave until cool enough to handle. Mash to a purée and leave to cool completely.

Put the potato in a bowl and beat in the egg yolks. Whisk in the olive oil, drop by drop to begin with, then in a thin stream, as for making mayonnaise. It may be necessary to thin the aïoli with a little cold water; the consistency should be like mayonnaise.

Add the garlic and anchovies and stir all together. Season with salt and pepper.

'good old
buttery
Brussels
sprouts,
topped with a
dusting of
freshly grated
Parmesan'

The Ultimate Christmas Chestnuts

3/4 stick (1/3 cup) unsalted butter
1 lb. vacuum-packed chestnuts
2 tablespoons brown sugar
1 large celeriac
2 1/2 cups good meat stock
A pinch of celery salt
Salt and freshly ground black pepper

This simple but delicious way of cooking chestnuts with celeriac was first shown to me by my friend and mentor Anton Mosimann during our time together at The Dorchester in London. I now regularly cook chestnuts like this at home over Christmas.

Heat the butter in a pan, add the chestnuts and sugar and cook for 8–10 minutes, until the chestnuts are lightly caramelized.

Peel the celeriac and grate it coarsely. Sprinkle it over the chestnuts and toss together. Pour in the stock, add a little salt, then bring to a boil. Reduce the heat and simmer until the stock forms a glaze around the chestnuts. Season with pepper and celery salt and serve.

PG TIPS I really see no need to prepare fresh chestnuts these days, since the quality of vacuum-packed and frozen ones is superb. However, if you do have time on your hands and prefer to use ones in the shell, simply score a cross in both rounded sides of each chestnut, ensuring you cut not only the tough outer shell but also the brown skin beneath. Bake in a hot oven for 45 minutes, then leave until just cool enough to handle before peeling.

Sweet and Sour Swiss Chard
with Cranberries

2 lb. Swiss chard
2 tablespoons unsalted butter
2 shallots, finely chopped
1/4 cup cranberry vinegar
2 tablespoons maple syrup
1/2 cup vegetable stock
2/3 cup cranberries
Salt and freshly ground black pepper

This is one of my favorite preparations during Christmas when fresh cranberries are available. The cranberry vinegar can be replaced with raspberry vinegar if necessary.

Remove the stalks from the chard and cut the leaves into 2-inch lengths. (To use the stalks, see Tip below.) Blanch the leaves in boiling salted water for 5–8 minutes, until just tender, then drain well.

Heat the butter in a pan, add the shallots and chard leaves and toss together. Add the cranberry vinegar, maple syrup and vegetable stock, then add the cranberries. Simmer rapidly until the liquid has reduced to a syrupy glaze, then season to taste and serve.

PG TIPS A delicious way to use up the chard stalks is to sauté them in olive oil with a little garlic, then toss with fresh pasta and season with balsamic vinegar.

Red Pepper Romesco Sauce

3 red peppers
3 plum tomatoes
2 green chiles, halved and
    seeded
2 garlic cloves, unpeeled
1 ancho chile
2/3 cup water
2 tablespoons red wine vinegar
2 tablespoons chopped fresh parsley
1 tablespoon smoked paprika
5 tablespoons olive oil
2 oz. blanched almonds, toasted
    and coarsely ground (to yield
    around 2/3 cup)
Salt and freshly ground black pepper

This spicy sauce from Spain is usually served with roasted lamb or pork but I also like to serve it with broiled eggplant and zucchini. It makes a good accompaniment to Escalivada (see page 37). In some parts of Spain I have seen it brushed on meat as a glaze.

Preheat the oven to 400°F. Place the peppers, tomatoes, green chiles and garlic cloves on a baking sheet and roast for 15–20 minutes, until blistered and soft. Leave to cool, then peel and seed the peppers and peel the garlic.

Put the ancho chile in a pan with the water and bring to a boil, then reduce the heat and simmer for 10 minutes.

Put the peppers, tomatoes, green chiles, garlic, ancho chile and its cooking water, vinegar, parsley and paprika in a blender or food processor and blitz until smooth. Add the oil while the machine is still running. Season to taste, then mix in the almonds. Store in the refrigerator if not using immediately; it will keep for 3–4 days.

PG TIPS Ancho chiles are dried poblano chiles. They tend to vary in heat. To use, soften them by soaking or simmering in hot water, then purée in a blender.

Cebollas en Adobo (Soused Pearl Onions with Ruby Vinegar and Raisins)

1 lb. small baby onions
2/3 cup red wine vinegar
1/2 cup red wine
1/2 cup olive oil
2 tablespoons sugar
1 cup water
1 bay leaf
1 sprig of fresh thyme
1/3 cup raisins
Salt and freshly ground black pepper

This Spanish-style dish is one of my favorite accompaniments to pâté or cold meats such as bresaola. It is also good served on its own as a starter.

Peel the onions (see Tip below) and trim the base but do not remove the root. Place the onions in a pan with all the remaining ingredients except the raisins and seasoning and bring to the boil. Add the raisins, reduce the heat and simmer for 1–1¼ hours, stirring frequently. When the onions are ready they should be tender and well glazed with the syrupy cooking liquid. Leave to cool, then season to taste. Remove the bay leaf and thyme before serving.

PG TIPS Peeling small onions or shallots is a tedious job. To make it easier, blanch the onions in boiling water for 1–2 minutes, then refresh in cold water. The skins are removed much more easily and with fewer tears!

Green Tomato and Pepper Chutney

Makes about 5 lbs.

**7 lbs. green tomatoes,
  seeded and cut into quarters**
1 onion, finely chopped
2 garlic cloves, crushed
**3 green peppers, seeded and
  chopped**
1/2 cup golden raisins
2 1/2 cups white wine vinegar
2/3 cup sugar
1/2 cup apple juice
2 teaspoons yellow mustard seeds
1 tablespoon cumin seeds
1 teaspoon ground tumeric
A pinch of chili powder
A pinch of ground cloves
1/2 cup olive oil

An ideal recipe for using up all those green tomatoes left at the end of the season. This chutney is delicious served with cold meat or with Spinach, Chile and Black Bean Fritters (see page 52).

Place all the ingredients in a preserving pan and heat until the sugar dissolves. Bring to a boil and simmer, stirring occasionally, for 1 hour or until thickened and syrupy. Leave to stand until cold, then pour into sterilized jars and seal. Store in a cool, dark place for at least two weeks before use and keep in the fridge once opened.

PG TIPS To sterilize jars, wash them thoroughly in hot soapy water, then rinse well and place on a baking tray. Dry in an oven preheated to 275°F.

Pickled Red Cabbage and Celery Seed Relish

1 small red cabbage, thinly shredded
2 celery stalks, thinly sliced
**1 green pepper, seeded and finely
  diced**
1/3 cup raisins
1/2 cup white wine vinegar
1/2 cup brown sugar
1 teaspoon celery seeds
1/2 teaspoon mustard seeds
1/2 cup peanut oil
1 teaspoon salt

Although you can buy pickled red cabbage, it does not compare with home-made. Be sure to leave the relish for a few days before using.

Put the cabbage, celery, green pepper and raisins in a large bowl.
  Boil together the vinegar, sugar, celery seeds and mustard seeds until the sugar has completely dissolved. Pour this mixture over the cabbage, add the oil and salt and stir to combine thoroughly. Leave in the fridge to marinate for 3–4 days or at least overnight. It will keep for about a month, or longer if stored in sterilized jars.

Turnip Sauerkraut

2 tablespoons black peppercorns

1 tablespoon Kosher or other coarse
    salt

12 juniper berries

3 lbs. large turnips, peeled and
    coarsely grated

1/4 cup duck fat or lard

1 onion, finely sliced

2 garlic cloves, crushed

1 tablespoon cumin seeds

4 1/2 oz. smoked ham (around 4
    slices), cut into lardons (short
    strips)

1 1/4 cups dry white wine

About 1 quart chicken stock

2 cooking apples, peeled, cored and
    grated

Salt and freshly ground black pepper

Sauerkraut, cabbage preserved in brine, is one of the world's most ancient foods. Here shredded turnip replaces the cabbage. I particularly like to serve this with game, such as pheasant or venison, or braised pork.

Mix together the peppercorns, salt and juniper berries. Arrange a layer of turnips in an earthenware crock or a large bowl and lightly sprinkle with a little of the salt mixture. Repeat these layers, ending with turnips. Cover with a clean cloth and a heavy weight, then leave overnight.

The next day, remove the juniper and peppercorns from the turnips, put the turnips in a colander and rinse thoroughly under cold water. Dry well in a cloth.

Preheat the oven to 325°F. Heat the duck fat or lard in a large casserole dish, add the onion, garlic and cumin seeds, and cook until the onion is golden. Add the smoked ham and cook for a few minutes longer, then stir in the turnips. Pour in the wine and enough chicken stock to cover the mixture by two thirds. Season with salt and pepper and cover with a lid. Transfer to the oven and cook for 1–1 1/2 hours, by which time the liquid should have evaporated. Stir in the apples and serve hot.

PG TIPS The sauerkraut will keep for 3-4 days in the refrigerator and in fact will taste all the better for it. Reheat with 2 tablespoons butter.

'celery marmalade with a tamarind twist - and why not?'

Celery and Tamarind Marmalade

1 stick (¹/₂ cup) unsalted butter
1 lb. celery hearts, thinly sliced
1 onion, thinly sliced
¹/₂ cup sugar
¹/₂ cup sherry vinegar
1 cup red wine
1 tablespoon tamarind paste
Salt and freshly ground black pepper

Tamarind, a popular ingredient in Indian cooking, is the sour-tasting pulp of a tropical tree. It is dried and then pressed into blocks, which need to be mixed with hot water and strained to give a paste before cooking. However, it is now also available bottled in paste form, which is much more convenient. Here is an unusual savory marmalade to accompany cooked meats. I serve it with foie gras, topped with cracked black pepper, but most cold meats would be suitable.

Heat the butter in a heavy-based pan until it begins to foam, add the celery and onion and season with salt and pepper. Stir in the sugar, cover the pan, then reduce the heat and cook for about 30–35 minutes, until the celery and onion become caramelized, stirring them occasionally. Uncover the pan, add the vinegar, red wine and tamarind and return to a low heat for 30 minutes, until the celery becomes slightly tacky in consistency, like marmalade. Serve hot or cold.

Preserved Elephant Garlic with Herbs

4 large heads of elephant garlic
2¹/₂ cups duck fat (or light olive oil)
4 sprigs of fresh thyme
2 sprigs of fresh marjoram
2 sprigs of fresh rosemary
2 bay leaves
Salt and freshly ground black pepper

Elephant garlic is a very large variety of garlic – about the size of an apple! The intense flavor of this superb garlic preparation makes it ideal for use in sauces, sautés and salads; simply scrape off excess fat and chop the garlic as normal. I also like to purée it to use in soups and pasta dishes, or to serve as an accompaniment to roast lamb.

Slice ¹/₈-inch off the top of each head of garlic to expose the cloves. Heat ¹/₄ cup of the duck fat in a heavy-based pan until very hot. Place the garlic heads cut-side down in the hot fat and cook for 1 minute, until caramelized. Turn them over, throw in the herbs and season with salt and pepper. Pour in the remaining duck fat and cook for about 25 minutes or until the garlic is very tender (it can also be cooked in a hot oven). Leave to cool. The garlic will keep in its fat for up to one month in the fridge.

chapter **four**

just desserts

Puddings don't immediately spring to mind when you think about cooking vegetables but why not? So many vegetables are rich in sugar that it seems only natural to exploit their sweetness in this way. If you're not convinced, just think of those eternally popular classic vegetable desserts, pumpkin pie and carrot cake. Before cane sugar became widely available in the eighteenth century, vegetables were a common sweetener.

In this chapter I've tried to show the versatility of vegetables with a range of sorbets and ice creams, plus a delicious aniseed-flavored fennel mousse (Fennel and Caramelized Banana Stacks, page 160), moist, dense Beet and Walnut Brownies (page 162) and even Iced Chestnut and Truffle Soufflés (page 163). Take these as a starting point for your own combinations – the possibilities are endless.

Carrot and Dried Fruit Pudding

Serves 6

²/₃ cup dates, diced
³/₄ cup dried figs, diced
3 tablespoons candied ginger, diced
1 cup boiling water
¹/₄ cup raisins
¹/₂ teaspoon baking soda
1 teaspoon baking powder
¹/₂ stick (¹/₄ cup) unsalted butter
¹/₄ cup sugar
2 eggs
1¹/₂ cups self-rising flour, sifted
1³/₄ cups coarsely grated carrots
¹/₂ teaspoon ground cinnamon
¹/₂ teaspoon ground mixed spice

Carrots have been used in sweet dishes for centuries and are a wonderful way of keeping cake mixtures moist. Here they are combined with sweet spices in a sumptuous baked pudding. Once you have tasted it you will want to make it again and again.

Preheat the oven to 375°F. Put the dates, figs and ginger in a bowl, then stir in the boiling water, raisins, baking soda and baking powder. Leave to stand for 15 minutes.

Beat the butter and sugar together until pale, then beat in the eggs one at a time. Fold in the flour, then stir in the dried fruit mixture, grated carrots and spices. Pour the mixture into 6 timbales or ramekins, 1-cup capacity, or into a 7-inch ovenproof dish. Place on a baking tray and bake for 30–35 minutes for individual puddings or 40–45 minutes for one large one, until they are risen and golden and a knife inserted in the center comes out clean. Leave for 5 minutes before tipping out.

Serve with heavy cream or fresh vanilla custard and a compote of dried fruits.

Corn Tostadas with Corn Ice Cream and Summer Berry Salsa

¹/₂ stick (¹/₄ cup) unsalted butter
¹/₄ cup sugar
2 tablespoons dark corn syrup
¹/₂ cup all purpose flour
¹/₂ teaspoon ground ginger
2¹/₃ cups cornflakes
Corn Ice Cream (see page 167)
¹/₃ cup white chocolate shavings

For the salsa:
¹/₃ cup each strawberries,
    raspberries and blackberries
1 tablespoon sugar
¹/₂ in. piece of fresh ginger,
    finely diced
1 tablespoon chopped fresh mint
5 tablespoons tequila

A fun play on Mexican tacos, made with cornflakes and filled with a delicate corn ice cream and a tequila and summer fruit salsa.

Preheat the oven to 350°F. For the tacos, melt the butter, sugar and syrup in a pan over a low heat. Remove from the heat and stir in the flour and ginger. Leave to cool slightly, then fold in the cornflakes. Place 4 large tablespoons of the mixture on a well-greased baking tray (allow plenty of room as they will spread) and bake for 8–10 minutes, until golden. Leave to cool for 30 seconds, then loosen each taco and quickly drap it over an upturned small dessert bowl or cup to shape it into a basket. Leave until cold and crisp, then carefully remove.

Halve the stawberries. Put the berries in a bowl, stir in the sugar, ginger and mint, then pour the tequila over them. Leave to marinate for 15 minutes.

To serve, fill the tacos with the corn ice cream, top with the fruit salsa and garnish with the chocolate shavings.

**'a crumbly
vegetable-
inspired
pudding,
enhanced
with sweet
spices'**

Sweet Potato
and Chèvre Cheesecake Strudel

1/2 lb. orange-fleshed sweet
 potatoes, peeled and cut into
 chunks (to yield around 2 cups)

3/4 stick (1/3 cup) unsalted butter

1/4 cup sugar

2 eggs, separated

Juice and grated zest of 1 lemon

2/3 cup ground almonds

1/4 lb. mild goat's cheese (around
 1/2 cup)

1/3 cup golden raisins

1/2 cup heavy cream

2 2/3 cups fresh white bread
 crumbs

3 large sheets of phyllo pastry
 dough, about 18 x 12 in.

1/2 stick (1/4 cup) unsalted butter,
 melted

Confectioners sugar for dusting

Sweet potatoes, as their name suggests, are high in sugar. Their sweetness balances the tangy goat's cheese perfectly.

Preheat the oven to 375°F. Cook the sweet potatoes in boiling water for about 20 minutes, until tender. Drain well and mash until smooth. Set aside.

Beat the butter and sugar together until pale and fluffy. Beat in the egg yolks one at a time, then add the lemon juice and zest, the almonds, goat's cheese, sweet potato purée and golden raisins. Finally mix in the cream and half the breadcrumbs. Whisk the egg whites until they form stiff peaks and fold them in.

Spread out one sheet of phyllo pastry dough on a flat surface and brush well all over with melted butter. Put a second sheet on top and butter again, then top with the third sheet. Brush with butter and sprinkle over the remaining breadcrumbs. Spread the filling on top, leaving a border of 1 1/4 inches all round the dough. Starting at a long side, roll up the dough and then seal the edges with a little melted butter. Grease a baking sheet with melted butter and place the strudel on it. Brush on the remaining butter and bake for 40–45 minutes, until golden and puffed. Remove and cool slightly, then dust liberally with confectioners sugar and serve.

PG TIPS When using phyllo pastry dough always work as quickly as possible, since it tends to dry out and become brittle if left exposed to the air for too long. Cover with a damp cloth if you are not using it immediately.

White Peach Tarts
with Tomato Jam, Lemon Sorbet

4 white peaches
A little brown sugar
4 scoops of good-quality lemon
  sorbet or sherbet
2 tablespoons sliced almonds,
  toasted

For the tomato jam:
1 lb., 5 oz. very ripe tomatoes
1 cup confectioners sugar

For the pastry dough:
2¼ cups all purpose flour
A pinch of salt
1 stick (½ cup) unsalted butter,
  diced (at room temperature)
¼ cup confectioners sugar, sifted
1 egg, beaten
1 egg, beaten with 1
  tablespoon water, to glaze

This recipe comes courtesy of chef Philippe Monti of the Hostellerie de Crillon de Brave in Provence. I love the tomato and lemon combination and I thank him for letting me include it in this book.

For the tomato jam, blanch the tomatoes in boiling water for 30 seconds, then peel them, cut them in half horizontally and remove the seeds. Chop the tomatoes very finely and place in a bowl. Stir in the sugar, cover and leave in the refrigerator overnight.

The next day, make the pastry dough: sift the flour and salt on to a work surface and make a well in the center. Put the butter and sugar in the well, then add the beaten egg. With your fingertips, gradually bring the flour into the center, blending in the butter, until all the ingredients come together into a dough. Knead very lightly for 1 minute, until completely smooth, then form the dough into a ball. Wrap in plastic wrap and leave to rest in the refrigerator for up to 1 hour.

Preheat the oven to 400°F. Roll out the dough very thinly and cut out 4 circles, each one 5 inches in diameter. Place on a baking sheet, then prick lightly with a fork, brush with a little of the beaten eggwash to glaze and bake until golden. Remove and leave to cool.

Drain the liquid from the tomatoes very thoroughly, put it in a pan and simmer over a low heat until it is reduced and syrupy. Put the tomatoes in the syrup and cook for 5 minutes, then remove from the heat and leave to cool. Spread the tomato jam on to the pastry rounds.

Blanch the peaches in boiling water for 1 minute, then remove with a slotted spoon and refresh in iced water. Peel the peaches, cut them in half and remove the pits. Thinly slice each half. Arrange the slices in a nice pattern on top of the tomato jam, leaving a space in the middle in which to put the lemon sorbet later. Sprinkle each tart with a little brown sugar and place under a preheated broiler until the sugar caramelizes.

To serve, place a scoop of lemon sorbet in the middle of each tart and sprinkle with the toasted almonds.

PG TIPS To ripen tomatoes at home, place them in a bag with a few holes pierced through and leave in a dark drawer. The natural gas in the tomatoes will speed up the process. Keep them away from direct sunlight.

'an unusual
combination
of leafy chard,
sweet, soft
pears and
lemony cheese'

Swiss Chard and Pear Tart

²/₃ cup golden raisins

2 tablespoons dark rum

2 lbs. Swiss chard, stalks
   removed (see Tips on page 146),
   leaves cooked and finely chopped

¹/₂ cup pine nuts

³/₄ cup confectioners sugar, plus
   extra for dusting

3 pears, peeled, cored and diced

3 tablespoons cream cheese

Grated zest of 1 lemon

2 eggs, beaten

For the pastry dough:

3 cups all purpose flour

2 sticks (1 cup) unsalted butter,
   diced (at room temperature)

A pinch of salt

1 cup confectioners sugar, sifted

Finely grated zest of ¹/₂ lemon

1 egg, beaten

This traditional dessert from Nice, an unusual combination of chard, fruit, pine nuts and cream cheese, is always served on feast days. Traditionally it is made with apples but I prefer pears. Serve with lashings of heavy cream.

For the pastry dough, sift the flour on to a work surface and make a well in the center. Put the butter, salt, sugar and lemon zest in the well and then add the egg. With your fingertips, gradually bring the flour into the center, blending in the butter, until all the ingredients come together into a soft dough. Knead very lightly for 1 minute, until completely smooth, then form the dough into a ball. Wrap in plastic wrap and leave to rest in the refrigerator for 1 hour.

Preheat the oven to 400°F. Roll out the dough and use to line a 9-inch fluted tart pan, reserving excess dough for the top. Prick the base with a fork and chill while you prepare the filling.

Soak the raisins in the rum for 15 minutes, then place in a saucepan and heat gently until all the liquid has been absorbed. Place the Swiss chard leaves in a bowl with the raisins and all the remaining ingredients. Mix well, then spread the filling in the pie shell and cover the top with the remaining pastry dough. Seal the edges and make a few vents in the top.

Bake for 45 minutes, until golden brown, then leave to cool. Turn out of the pan, dust with confectioners sugar and serve.

PG TIPS If you do not have time to make the dough, you can now buy some good-quality pre-baked pie shells. Use the same filling but top with buttered phyllo pastry dough.

Fennel and Caramelized Banana Stacks

1/2 stick (1/4 cup) unsalted butter, melted

8 sheets of phyllo pastry dough

1/4 cup confectioners sugar, plus extra for dusting

For the fennel mousse:

1 large fennel bulb, chopped

1/4 cup sugar

4 egg yolks

2 tablespoons custard powder (or, if unavailable, use cornstarch)

1/4 vanilla bean

1/4 cup Marie Brizard (or other anise liquor such as Pernod)

2 tablespoons heavy cream, semi-whipped

For the caramelized bananas:

1/2 cup sugar

3 large bananas, peeled and cut into slices 3/4 in. thick

1/3 cup Marie Brizard (or other anise liquor such as Pernod)

First prepare the phyllo stacks. Preheat the oven to 350°F. Lightly brush a baking sheet with a little of the melted butter. Place one sheet of phyllo on a work surface, brush with melted butter, then place another sheet on top. Brush with butter and sprinkle with a tablespoon of the confectioners sugar. Top with another sheet of phyllo and brush with butter. Place the fourth sheet on top, brush with butter and sprinkle with a tablespoon of confectioners sugar. Repeat with the remaining 4 sheets so you have 2 separate piles. Cut out six 3-inch circles from each phyllo stack, place on the prepared baking sheet and bake for 5–7 minutes or until golden brown. Remove from the oven and leave to cool.

For the fennel mousse, put the fennel in a pan, add 2 tablespoons of the sugar and just enough water to cover. Bring to a boil, then reduce the heat and simmer for 20–25 minutes or until very tender. Transfer to a blender and blitz to a purée (you will need approximately 1/2 cup purée). Put the egg yolks, the remaining sugar and the custard powder in a bowl and whisk until smooth. Slit the vanilla bean open lengthways and scrape out the seeds. Heat the fennel purée, Marie Brizard and vanilla seeds in a pan and then carefully pour on to the egg mixture, whisking as you do so. Return to the pan and cook for 3–4 minutes, stirring constantly, until thickened. Transfer to a large bowl and leave to cool, then whisk until smooth. Fold in the whipped cream.

For the caramelized bananas, heat the sugar in a heavy-based frying pan over a high heat until it dissolves and forms a caramel. Add the bananas and cook for 1 minute. Pour in the Marie Brizard to form a light anise caramel. Leave to cool.

To assemble, place a phyllo circle in the center of each serving plate, place a heaped spoonful of fennel mousse in the center and top with some caramelized banana. Put another phyllo circle on top and repeat the layers of fennel mousse and banana. Top with a third phyllo circle. Dust with a little confectioners sugar, pour some of the caramel around it and serve immediately.

'crisp phyllo discs with layers of sweet anise filling'

Pumpkin Beignets Soufflés with Bourbon Honey Sabayon

¹/₂ cup golden raisins
5 tablespoons bourbon
1 lb. pumpkin, peeled and cut
   into chunks
¹/₂ stick unsalted butter, melted
¹/₄ cup sugar
1 cup self-rising flour, sifted
Grated zest of ¹/₂ orange
2 eggs, separated
¹/₂ teaspoon ground allspice
2 teaspoons ground cinnamon
Vegetable oil for deep-frying

For the sabayon:
3 egg yolks
¹/₄ cup honey
5 tablespoons bourbon
2 tablespoons water
¹/₄ cup orange juice

Preheat the oven to 400°F. Soak the golden raisins in the bourbon for up to 1 hour, then drain well and dry them.

Place the pumpkin on a large piece of foil, pour over it the melted butter and seal up the foil. Place in the oven for 30 minutes or until soft, then transfer to a bowl and mash to a smooth purée. Add half the sugar, the flour, orange zest, soaked raisins, egg yolks, allspice and half the cinnamon, and mix well. In a separate bowl, whisk the egg whites until they form stiff peaks. Fold them into the pumpkin mixture.

Mix the remaining sugar and cinnamon together and set aside. Heat the vegetable oil in a pan or a deep-fat fryer to 350°F. Using a large spoon, drop spoonfuls of the mixture into the oil and fry until crisp and golden. Drain the beignets on kitchen paper, then toss with the sugar and cinnamon mixture. Keep warm.

For the sabayon, place all the ingredients in the top of a double broiler, or in a bowl set over a pan of simmering water, ensuring that the base of the bowl does not touch the water. Whisk continuously until light and fluffy and doubled in volume; the mixture should be thick. Serve immediately, with the beignets.

Wicked Beet and Walnut Brownies

Serves 6–8

2 sticks (1 cup) unsalted butter
11 oz. dark chocolate
3 eggs
1 cup sugar
¹/₄ lb. beets, cooked and puréed
   (to yield around ¹/₂ cup)
¹/₄ cup raspberry liquor
1 cup chopped walnuts
³/₄ cup, plus 2 tablespoons all
   purpose flour, sifted

A classic American brownie with the added crunch of walnuts and the sweetness of puréed beets and raspberry liquor. The beets help keep the chocolate base moist and add a vibrant color.

Preheat the oven to 375°F. Melt the butter and chocolate in the top of a double broiler, or in a bowl set over a pan of simmering water, making sure the base of the bowl does not touch the water. Put the eggs and sugar in a mixing bowl and beat until light and creamy. Stir in the melted butter and chocolate. Add the beet purée, raspberry liquor and walnuts, then fold in the flour. Pour the brownie mixture into a well-buttered baking pan, approximately 11 x 7 inches. Bake for 25–30 minutes, then remove from the oven and leave to cool. Turn out on to a wire rack and cut into squares. Serve with cream or vanilla ice cream.

PG TIPS Be careful not to overcook the brownies or they will be dry.

Iced Chestnut
and Truffle Soufflés

2 eggs, separated
¹/₄ cup sugar
2 tablespoons port or rum
a generous ¹/₂ cup unsweetened
**   chestnut purée**
¹/₄ cup truffle juice
1 cup heavy cream, semi-whipped
1 small fresh (or canned) black
**   truffle, roughly chopped (optional)**
¹/₂ cup marrons glacés, roughly
**   chopped**

To decorate:
A little whipped cream
4 marrons glacés

Chestnuts and truffles have a natural affinity and their wintry flavors work well together in hot dishes. Here, for a change, I have combined them in delicate iced soufflés. A simple chocolate sauce would go very well with them. Use a fresh truffle if possible but canned will do.

Take four ¹/₂-cup soufflé dishes and wrap a double thickness of lightly oiled wax paper around each one so that it comes 1 inch above the rim. Secure with scotch tape. Place the egg yolks, sugar and port or rum in the top of a double broiler, or in a bowl set over a pan of simmering water, making sure the base of the bowl does not touch the water. Whisk the mixture until it is pale, thick and creamy and has doubled in volume. Remove the bowl from the pan and continue to whisk until the mixture is cold.

Mix together the chestnut purée and truffle juice and warm them slightly. Fold them into the egg yolk mixture, ensuring there are no lumps. Gently fold in the cream, then the truffle and marrons glacés. Whip the egg whites until stiff and fold them into the mixture. Pour the mixture into the soufflé dishes and place in the freezer for about 4 hours, until frozen. Remove from the freezer, carefully unpeel the paper and decorate each soufflé with whipped cream and a whole marron glacé.

PG TIPS Truffle juice is available from good delicatessens, or you could use the juice from a canned truffle.

Coconut Milk, Yoghurt and Red Chile Sorbet

1 small hot red chile
2 cups sugar
2 cups water
14-oz. can of unsweetened coconut milk
1 cup plain yoghurt
1/4 cup white rum

This is a very good example of the way in which vegetables can give a special flavor to desserts: I love this recipe because it adds a touch of unexpected spice.

Cut the chile in half lengthways, remove the seeds and dice very finely. Place in a pan with the sugar and water, bring to a boil and simmer for 1–1 1/2 minutes or until the sugar has completely dissolved. Remove from the heat and stir in the coconut milk, yoghurt and rum. Leave to cool.

Pour into a sorbetière and freeze until firm, following the manufacturer's instructions. If you don't have a sorbetière, pour the mixture into a bowl and place in the freezer. After 30 minutes, when the mixture is beginning to set, remove it from the freezer and beat well with an electric beater or hand blender to disperse any ice crystals, then return it to the freezer. Repeat this 2 or 3 times, then leave until the sorbet is set firm.

PG TIPS In general, the smaller the chile, the hotter it is. Always buy chiles that are firm to the touch. Once they become soft, they lose their fresh flavor.

Butternut Squash and Orange Sorbet

2 cups sugar
2 cups water
1 lb. butternut squash, peeled and finely chopped
1 1/2 cups fresh orange juice
5 tablespoons Grand Marnier (optional)

Butternut squash and orange bring out the best in each other when combined in a simple recipe like this.

Bring the sugar and water to a boil and simmer for 1–1 1/2 minutes or until the sugar has completely dissolved. Remove from the heat and set aside. Put the butternut squash and orange juice in a separate pan and cook until the squash is soft and pulpy. Transfer to a blender, add the sugar syrup and blitz to a smooth purée. Strain through a fine strainer and add the Grand Marnier, if using.

Pour into a sorbetière and freeze until firm, following the manufacturer's instructions. If you don't have a sorbetière, pour the mixture into a bowl and place in the freezer. After 30 minutes, when the mixture is beginning to set, remove it from the freezer and beat well with an electric beater or hand blender to disperse any ice crystals, then return it to the freezer. Repeat this 2 or 3 times, then leave until the sorbet is set firm.

'right at the
heart of its
icy coolness
lurks the
unmistakable
hint of hot
chiles'

Caramelized Onion
and Balsamic Ice Cream

1/2 cup thinly sliced onions
2 tablespoons unsalted butter
1/2 cup sugar
2/3 cup red wine
Juice and grated zest of 1 orange
4 egg yolks
1 egg
2 cups milk
1/2 cup heavy cream
1 tablespoon balsamic vinegar

Caramelizing onions brings out their natural sweetness, while the balsamic vinegar adds a tart, sweet note. Together they create perfect harmony, a sweet and slightly sour ice cream that I regularly prepare at home for dinner parties. It certainly makes a good conversation piece!

Put the onions in a pan of boiling water, simmer for 5 minutes, then drain. Repeat, then dry well on a kitchen towel. Melt the butter and half of the sugar gently in a pan, add the onions and cook for 15 minutes, stirring occasionally, until caramelized to a deep brown color. Add the red wine, orange juice and zest and boil until reduced by half.

Whisk the egg yolks, whole egg and the remaining sugar together until the mixture whitens. Put the milk, cream and onions in a clean pan and bring to a boil, then pour on to the egg mixture a little at a time, stirring. Return to a clean pan and cook over a gentle heat, stirring all the time with a wooden spoon, until the mixture is thick enough to coat the back of the spoon. Be careful not to let it boil.

Strain the mixture into a clean bowl and stir in the balsamic vinegar. Cool the ice cream quickly by standing the bowl in a larger bowl of iced water and stirring until cold. Churn in an ice-cream maker until the mixture resembles semi-whipped cream, then freeze until firm. If you don't have an ice-cream maker, pour the mixture into a bowl and place in the freezer. After 30 minutes, when the mixture is beginning to set, remove from the freezer and beat well with an electric beater or hand blender to disperse any ice crystals, then return it to the freezer. Repeat this 2 or 3 times, then leave until the ice cream is set firm.

PG TIPS Blanching the onions in boiling water is an important step in making this ice cream. It removes the acid from them and any bitterness, too.

Fennel, Raisin and Saffron Ice Cream

1/4 lb. fennel

1 tablespoon unsalted butter

1/4 cup sugar

1 tablespoon Marie Brizard (or other anise liquor such as Pernod)

1/3 cup raisins

4 egg yolks

1 egg

2 cups whole milk

1/2 cup heavy cream

2 pinches of saffron strands

1 star anise

Serve with poached pears or figs or a warm apple tart.

Chop the fennel into small dice, about the same size as a raisin. Cook gently with the butter and half of the sugar for 8 minutes or until soft. Warm the Marie Brizard, pour it over the raisins and leave for 15 minutes. Add the fennel and set aside.

Whisk the egg yolks, whole egg and the remaining sugar together until the mixture whitens. Put the milk, cream, saffron and star anise in a pan and bring to a boil. Pour on to the egg mixture a little at a time, stirring. Return to a clean pan and cook over a gentle heat, stirring all the time with a wooden spoon, until the mixture is thick enough to coat the back of the spoon. Be careful not to let it boil.

Strain the mixture into a clean bowl, then stir in the fennel mixture. Cool the ice cream quickly by standing the bowl in a larger bowl of iced water and stirring until cold. Churn in an ice-cream maker until the mixture resembles semi-whipped cream, then freeze until firm. If you don't have an ice-cream maker, pour the mixture into a bowl and place in the freezer. After 30 minutes, when the mixture is beginning to set, remove from the freezer and beat with an electric beater or hand blender to disperse any ice crystals, then return it to the freezer. Repeat 2 or 3 times, then leave until the ice cream is set firm.

Corn Ice Cream

3 egg yolks

1 egg

2/3 cup sugar

2 cups milk

1 cup heavy cream

3/4 cup canned corn, puréed

Whisk the egg yolks, whole egg and sugar together until pale in color and doubled in volume. Put the milk and cream in a pan and bring to a boil. Pour a little at a time on to the egg mixture, stirring all the time. Add the puréed corn and strain through a strainer.

Return the mixture to a clean pan and cook over a low heat, stirring constantly with a wooden spoon, until the mixture thickens enough to coat the back of the spoon. Be careful not to let it boil.

Cool the ice cream quickly by standing the bowl in a larger bowl of iced water and stirring until cold. Churn in an ice-cream maker until the mixture resembles semi-whipped cream, then freeze until firm. If you don't have an ice-cream maker, pour the mixture into a bowl and place in the freezer. After 30 minutes, when the mixture is beginning to set, remove from the freezer and beat well with an electric beater or hand blender to disperse any ice crystals, then return it to the freezer. Repeat this 2 or 3 times, then leave until the ice cream is set firm

s q u a s h e s

A collection of squashes is the perfect candidate for a still life. With their fantastical shapes and vastly differing sizes, their netted, smooth or scalloped surface and beautiful, muted colors, they look almost too lovely to eat. Until recently, pumpkins, marrows and zucchini were all you could buy in the UK but now the whole glorious family of gourds is available, from the tiny, scalloped, pale-green or yellow pattypan to the chubby, brightly colored spaghetti squash with its fragile, stringy flesh. In their native America, squashes have been enjoyed for centuries but once English settlers brought the seeds back to Europe they quickly became established on this side of the Atlantic, too. The

Chayote (left)

English adopted the clumsy, overgrown marrow; the Italians and French had the good sense to eat the same vegetable while still tiny, tender and sweet, christening it zucchini and courgette respectively. Pumpkins are popular everywhere, used to make thick soups, casseroles, pies and gratins and even puréed as a filling for pasta. In the Middle East they are often combined with sweet and sour flavorings or candied as a rich dessert.

Although most squashes are now grown all year round, they are generally divided into summer and winter varieties. Summer squashes, such as zucchini, pattypan, crookneck squash and chayote, have thin skins and soft seeds and can be eaten whole. Winter ones have been matured on the plant until much larger and their tough skin and hard seeds must be discarded before eating. Pumpkin is the best known winter squash, but others include acorn, butternut, hubbard, spaghetti and turban squashes.

The one thing they all have in common is their sweetish, rather bland flavor, which makes them the most adaptable of vegetables. They go well with spices, herbs, garlic, tomatoes, cheese and sweet and sour combinations, and, of course, are wonderful in desserts, such as the classic American pumpkin pie.

Acorn squash

Chayote
   (also chow-chow or
   christophine)

Butternut squash

Crookneck squash

Gemsquash

Kabocha squash

Patty pan squash

Spaghetti squash

Zucchini

Pumpkins

Turks turban

arugula There's no mistaking the strong, peppery flavor of arugula, also known as rocket. Occasionally you may come across wild arugula in the shops, which has longer, spikier leaves and an even more powerful taste. Although arugula is readily available in supermarkets, packets tend to be small – it's packaged like an herb rather than a salad leaf –and prices high. Greek greengrocer's often sell large bunches, which are great for cooking with. Alternatively, if you invest in a packet of seeds, arugula is easily established in the garden.

Like all leaves, arugula is fragile and should be eaten as soon as possible. Discard any yellowing leaves or tough stalks.

asparagus Asparagus is now available year-round as an import but there's nothing to beat the flavor of freshly picked homegrown asparagus, in season in late spring. Green asparagus is usually grown in the UK while the French and Italians prefer a fatter white variety. Very young, slender green shoots are known as sprue and are often sold more cheaply – a bonus for the cook. When buying, look for firm spears with tightly closed tips and no wrinkles. To prepare, trim each spear by snapping off the white woody part, then peel away the skin from the base towards the top. The amount you will need to remove depends upon the quality and freshness of the asparagus; thin varieties may only need trimming.

beets I've always been fond of beets and have never understood why it is so often served with acidic dressings that mask its natural sweetness. Happily, inventive cooks have started to take an interest in it, serving it up in more flattering ways such as roasted or raw, as a pasta filling, a relish or even in a cake.

Always buy beets raw. Small, firm ones have the best flavor and if the leaves are still attached they should be green and fresh. Trim off the leafy tops and store in a cool, dark place. Before cooking, trim the stalks and wash well, being careful not to break the skin or the beets will bleed.

cardoon Unlike its famous relative the artichoke, the cardoon is not highly regarded in the UK. In France, Spain and Italy, however, this giant vegetable is prized for its delicate flavor, similar to artichokes or celery but more muted. It is shaped like a celery head, too, with thick, white stalks and leafy tops. When buying, try to avoid hollow stalks, as these will be dry and tough. Cardoons keep well in the fridge for several days. To prepare, trim off the leaves and any spikes, then pull off the strings, as for celery, and peel off the inner white skin. Cut the stalks into short lengths and put into water acidulated with lemon juice to prevent browning.

celeriac Celeriac or celery root is a type of celery but it is the root that is eaten rather than the stalks. This gnarled, misshapen globe is not the most beautiful of vegetables but if you dislike the stringiness of celery, celeriac, with its mellow, nutty flavor, is a more palatable alternative. Choose small, firm celeriac (large ones can be woody) with as smooth a skin as possible to make peeling easier. It should keep in the fridge for a couple of weeks. To prepare, trim the ends, peel off the thick skin, then either use immediately or put in water acidulated with lemon juice to prevent discoloration.

chayote Also known as chow-chow or christophine, this ridged, pale-green, avocado-shaped vegetable belongs to the squash family. It is popular in the Caribbean, and its bland flesh combines well with the spicy stews of that region. It is also a useful vegetable for stuffing and baking.

Choose small, firm chayote and store in the fridge, where they should keep for several weeks. Both the skin and the central seed are edible, although I prefer to peel them for stews.

chicory and endive Strictly speaking, these two plants belong to the genus *Cichorium*, and comprise a whole family of salad vegetables, which includes blanched endive (called Belgian endive in the US, but chicory and witloof in the UK); curly endive (often referred to as chicory in the US); broad-leaved endive (called escarole in the US, and batavia in the UK); and the red-leaved radicchio. Belgian endive, also known as French endive and

witloof chicory, refers specifi-
cally to the slim, tightly-
packed, tapering heads of
pale, yellowish-white leaves.
This type of endive was
'invented' by the Belgians
(hence, 'Belgian endive'), by
cutting off the tops and forcing
the roots in darkness so the
white tips appear. (The
Belgians and French call this
vegetable endive, while
chicorée is their name for
what the British call curly
endive or *frisée*. The
Americans side with the
French, using the word
chicory for the loose-headed,
curly-leaved vegetable, and
'Belgian endive' for the
blanched spears. There is a
variety of red chicory, too,
which is less commonly available but worth looking for.)
With its characteristic bitter
flavor and crisp texture, the
Belgian endive makes an
interesting addition to salads,
but is also very good braised.
Choose pale, tightly-closed,
yellow-tipped heads – without
any sign of green or they will
be too bitter – and check that
the stalk end hasn't turned
brown. Store in the fridge for
up to two days. To prepare,
trim the stalk end, then separate the leaves, if using for
salads, or if cooking, cut in half
lengthways or leave whole.

**chinese flowering
cabbage** Flowering cab-
bage, or choi sum (see pic),
has a delicate prettiness quite
unlike our solid, round native
cabbages. Its pale stalks are
topped by tender green
leaves and small yellow
flowers rather like cowslips.
Although the stems have the
best flavor – delicate, sweet
and only slightly cabbagey –
the leaves are used too.

Buy tender, fresh, bright-
green stems in flower, with
crisp stalks, and use within a
couple of days. Simply wash
and trim if necessary before
use. Small heads can be
cooked whole.

corn The story goes that
you should have the water
boiling for corn before you
pick it if you want to enjoy it at
its sweet, succulent best.
Since this is impossible for
most of us, it's lucky that new
varieties have been developed
where the sugar doesn't turn
to starch so quickly – although
you should still eat it as fresh
as possible. When buying corn
on the cob, look for plump
specimens with tightly packed
kernels and a soft, fresh husk
if this is still attached. Simply
cook whole in boiling water,
then stand the cob upright
and slice off the kernels if the
recipe requires it.
Baby corn looks pretty but
isn't overendowed with flavor.
Canned and frozen are useful
standbys, if a little oversweet.

eggplant Besides the
familiar long, shiny, purple
eggplants, you can also buy
white, yellow and green ones
in varying shapes, some as
small as peas. Whichever sort
you buy, they should be firm,
unwrinkled and heavy for their
size. Store in a cool, dark
place for up to three days.
Salting used to be recom-
mended to prevent bitterness
but this isn't generally necessary with modern varieties.
However, salting will reduce the
amount of oil the eggplants
soak up, so if you are frying
them you might prefer to slice
or dice and salt them first.
Leave in a colander for 30 minutes to 1 hour, then rinse and
pat dry.

fava beans Fava or
broad beans have been cultivated since the Bronze Age are

still a popular crop among gardeners. Growing them yourself means you can enjoy the tiny, tender first beans of the season – good eaten raw, with cheese or cured meat. Avoid any wrinkled, yellowing pods or the beans will be tough and coarse. Store in a bag in the fridge and shell just before cooking. Frozen beans make a good substitute for fresh. Whichever, it is worth taking the trouble to peel off the pale grey inner skin after cooking to reveal the brilliant-green little bean inside.

fennel Bulb, or Florence, fennel looks like a squat celery but there is also a leafier plant, grown as an herb and for its seeds, which has long, thin stalks. Both are natives of Italy, and fennel has a real affinity with Italian flavorings. Its sweet, aniseedy taste can be pungent when raw but mellows with cooking.

Choose plump, firm bulbs that are heavy for their size and store in the fridge for up to three days. Before cooking, trim the base, cut off the hard stalks (the feathery fronds can be reserved for garnish) and remove any stringy or damaged outer layers.

globe artichoke This edible thistle is such a bizarre and labor-intensive vegetable that you wonder how it ever occured to anyone to eat it. Once they have tackled an artichoke successfully though, most people are won over by its delicate yet distinctive flavor.

Artichokes are available in various shades of green and purple. Choose firm specimens with tightly closed leaves and a stem that looks freshly cut. Ideally, eat on the day of purchase. To prepare, snap off the stalk, pulling away any tough fibers with it, then pull off all the fibrous, dark-green outer leaves until you reach the tender, yellowish-green inner leaves. Cut off one to two thirds from the top of the artichoke, depending on how pale, and thus tender, the leaves are. With a paring knife, trim the dark-green exterior of the base, rubbing the exposed parts with a squeezed lemon half to prevent discoloration, then trim off any remaining dark-green leaves. Once all the external leaves are removed you will see the tightly packed central leaves concealing the hairy choke. Either scoop out the raw choke with a teaspoon or (which is easier) remove it after boiling. Drop the artichokes into a large bowl of water acidulated with lemon juice as you prepare them, as they discolor quickly.

In Italy and northern France tiny artichokes (known as poivrade) are picked before the choke has formed and can be eaten whole – even raw. A delicious way of enjoying artichokes without going to the bother of preparing them.

japanese artichoike Japanese artichokes, or crosnes, are hard to find in the UK but if you do happen to see them, snap them up. These small, spiral tubers have a delicious flavor, not unlike Jerusalem artichokes, and are easy to prepare. Choose plump, firm ones without any discolorations. Store in the fridge for no more than three days, then top and tail and wash well before use. If you want to remove the thin skins, blanch the artichokes in boiling water, then rub gently in a lint free towel with a little coarse salt. Rinse and pat dry.

jerusalem artichoke These small, misshapen tubers are related to the sunflower rather than the globe artichoke, despite their vaguely similar flavor. They are available in the winter and their crisp, transluscent flesh is good roasted or mashed, used in soups and gratins or even sliced thinly and eaten raw.

Choose firm artichokes that are as regularly shaped as possible to make peeling easier. To prevent discoloration, peel quickly and then drop into water acidulated with lemon juice. Very knobbly ones are easier to peel after boiling.

mushrooms The choice of cultivated mushrooms in the shops is increasing all the time. Button mushrooms are useful for their white flesh, which doesn't discolor sauces, but for flavor I prefer the more meaty portabello, chestnut and field mushroooms. Wild mushrooms are expensive but delicious, and their flavors are so intense that just a few can be used to liven up a dish of cultivated mushrooms.

When buying mushrooms, look for firm specimens that smell fresh and are neither withered nor waterlogged. Store in the fridge in a paper bag with a few air holes in it and use within two or three days.

To clean, wipe with a damp cloth, or rinse quickly under the cold tap if very dirty, and trim the stalk end. Some wild mushrooms require special treatment. Morels tend to trap the dirt, so wash them gently but thoroughly in cold water, then cut off the stem. I like to make a small slit in the side of each morel to release any sand trapped inside. Chanterelles, too, can be very dirty, so wash them several times in cold water, then dry well on a cloth. Porcini should never be washed in water, as they soak it up like a sponge, ruining their delicate flavor. Simply clean them with a damp cloth or soft brush before slicing them thinly.

okra These long, tapering, five-sided pods, also known as ladies' fingers, have an elegant appearance but exude a most inelegant slime when cooked. Don't be alarmed – it's this sticky liquid that enriches American gumbo and Indian and Caribbean stews. Make sure the okra you buy are crisp and fresh, without any brown patches; they should keep for several days in a plastic bag in the fridge. Wash well, then trim the stalk end, being careful not to expose the seeds. Some recipes recommend salting okra in acidulated water before cooking but I have never found this necessary.

salsify This looks like a long, skinny carrot, with a rough, brownish skin and crisp, pale flesh. It's a shame it's not more popular as it makes a useful vegetable for the winter months and has a subtle, interesting flavor – good in soups, gratins and even fritters. Choose smooth, hard specimens and store in

the fridge or a cool, dark place. To prevent discoloration when preparing, either peel and drop into acidulated water before cooking or cook in their skins and then peel.

sorrel Sorrel looks like spinach and cooks like spinach but has a wonderful tart, lemony flavor that is good in sauces or, if the leaves are young and tender, added to salads in small quantities. It's not always easy to find, although some supermarkets are now stocking it and it grows well in the garden. Sorrel has a short shelf life, so use as quickly as possible. Prepare as for spinach and, if you are cooking it, don't be disappointed when it turns into a dull green sludge – this makes a delicious and easy sauce for fish or eggs when enriched with cream or butter.

spinach When buying spinach choose bright, bouncy-fresh leaves and remember that it cooks down to almost nothing, so you always need much more than you expect. Store in a cool, dark place and use within two days. Large-leafed spinach sold loose needs a thorough wash to remove dirt and grit. Discard tough stalks or any damaged leaves. Supermarkets now sell bags of tender young spinach

leaves which, though pricy, have the advantage of not needing much preparation. Baby spinach is sold at a premium to use in salads. However, size isn't necessarily a guide to quality; large leaves can be succulent and full-flavored and are usually the best bet for cooking. Frozen spinach is best reserved for emergencies, but is also good used in stuffings and fillings.

squash The range of squashes available in the UK is improving all the time, although we still don't have anything like the variety on sale in America. Squashes are generally divided into winter and summer types, despite the fact that most of them are now on sale all year round. Winter squashes such as pumpkin, butternut and acorn have hard, inedible skins and need peeling and seeding before eating. Summer squashes such as zucchini and pattypan are more delicate and can be eaten whole. When buying squash, choose firm, unwrinkled specimens that are heavy for their size. Summer squash should not be limp and flabby. Winter varieties have the advantage of a long shelflife and will keep for many weeks in a cool place, whereas summer squash should be stored in the fridge and used within four days.

sweet potato Here's a vegetable for the sweet-toothed. Its rich, chestnutty sweetness almost verges on cloying, but it is surprisingly good with chiles and spices. The orange variety has moister flesh, while the white ones can be rather mealy. Sweet potatoes are not related to potatoes at all but are generally prepared in the same way. When buying, check the color of the flesh by scraping away a tiny patch of skin with your fingernail. They should keep for a few weeks in a cool, dark place and can be peeled and boiled like potatoes, but often have a better flavor if baked or boiled whole in their skins.

swiss chard Swiss chard is a type of beet and has the wonderfully economic virtue of being two vegetables in one: the dark-green leaves and the juicy white stalks, or ribs. Cook the leaves in the same way as spinach. The sweeter, more delicate-tasting ribs can be steamed or poached and served with melted butter or a sauce. When buying chard, look for crisp leaves and firm stalks without any brown patches.

index

ackowledgements

As with most projects, the creation of this book has been very much a team effort rather than the concentrated effort of one person. I would therefore like to thank the following people:

Jane Middleton, editor, whose invaluable friendship and advice helped turn my recipes and aspirations into print. Louise Pickford and Jane Stevenson for preparing the food for the camera with such artistic skill. Gus Filgate, photographer, for providing such superb food images.

Lara King, my PA not only for organizing me, but for fine-tuning my recipes. Fiona Lindsey and Linda Shanks, my agents, for their friendship and support. My kitchen brigade for their daily hard work and commitment to excellence. Kate Oldfield, project editor, Kyle and all my friends at Kyle

Cathie who shared my vision and without who's effort and enthusiasm this book would not have been possible. Finally, a special note of appreciation goes to Geoffrey Gelardi, Managing Director of The Lanesborough, and to Rosewood Hotels and Resorts for their continuing support of my work.